Lone Wolf

Lone Wolf

The Remarkable Story of Britain's Greatest
Nightfighter Ace of the Blitz – Flight Lieutenant
Richard Playne Stevens DSO, DFC & Bar

Andy Saunders with Terry Thompson

GRUB STREET · LONDON

Published by
Grub Street
4 Rainham Close
London SW11 6SS

Copyright © Grub Street 2019
Copyright text © Andy Saunders 2019

A CIP record for this title is available from the British library

ISBN-13: 978-1-911621-34-8

Design by Lucy Thorne

Printed and bound by Finidr in the Czech Republic

Contents

DEDICATION

To my late friend and colleague, Terry Thompson

The author hopes that this volume will shine an accurate spotlight on a man and his deeds; a man who equally deserves, with his more universally known contemporaries, to be properly, accurately and appropriately remembered.

NOTE ON SOURCES

The primary source of all information used in the compilation of this book was the extensive archive of research material built up across nearly 30 years by the late Terry Thompson.

This archive comprised original material donated by surviving members of the Stevens family, as well as interview notes, letters and tape recordings etc. drawn from those who either knew Richard Playne Stevens or served with him, as well as those who had specialist or specific knowledge to aid the project.

The archive also includes copies of official documentation, such as relevant extracts from RAF operations record books, German archival sources etc.

The author intends that Terry Thompson's R P Stevens archive will ultimately be deposited with a national repository or facility and be available in the public domain for future study.

FOREWORD

Flight Lieutenant Richard Stevens was probably the only successful nightfighter pilot who achieved success at night solely by the use of his own eyes.

My successes at night were almost entirely due to the use of radar and an operator, as my own night vision capability was not exceptional. As I had achieved some of the earliest successful interceptions at night, the Air Ministry decided that, for security reasons, and not to let it be known that we had radar in our nightfighters, they would encourage the belief that I had exceptional night vision. I had to accept this explanation of my success in the interests of security.

As a consequence, the press named me 'Cat's Eyes'. However, it was Stevens – and not me – who was unique in being the only really successful 'Cat's Eyes' nightfighter pilot in the whole of the Royal Air Force.

Group Captain John Cunningham
CBE, DSO & 2 bars, DFC & bar

Group Captain John Cunningham.

Note: During the initial research work for this book, Group Captain John Cunningham, one of the foremost nightfighter pilots of the Second World War, was contacted in relation to Richard Stevens and asked to provide a foreword for what was, then, an unwritten book.

Group Captain Cunningham readily agreed and penned this appreciation of the original 'Cat's Eyes' pilot, expressing the desire that his tribute to Richard Stevens would ultimately be published. Group Captain Cunningham died on 21 July 2002.

Introduction

In the summer of 1986, I had a chance meeting with the late Terry Thompson. That meeting led to a friendship across some 30 years. It also led to this book being written.

Terry, an avid aviation enthusiast and historical researcher, asked me soon after our meeting whether there were any well-known RAF 'aces' who had never been properly researched or written about. When I told him: 'Yes, Richard Playne Stevens!' he immediately set to and began a research project which spanned more than 25 years. Setting out on his journey, the long-term ambition was to see the fruits of his research eventually published.

The result was truly astonishing, and Terry managed to track down what must have been every surviving piece of information which existed on Richard Stevens. Apart from family members, and those who had flown with him, Terry located an extraordinary amount of detail about Richard's astonishing yet little-known RAF career. During the course of his work it would be true to say that his diligence left no stone unturned. His research was a masterpiece. Without doubt, he assembled the most remarkable archive I have ever seen on a single RAF pilot. Whilst that should have been a blessing to any author, it conversely became something of a two-edged sword; such was the bulk of material that it was difficult to see the wood from the trees when assembling this book.

Sadly, Terry did not live to see the eventual fruition of his work come to life in the pages of *Lone Wolf*. However, after he had moved house, Terry deposited with me his archive saying that he had got as far as he could. Now, he didn't quite know where to go with what he had pulled together.

In giving me the archive, Terry wanted me to see if I could somehow make use of it. I told him that it formed the basis of a wonderful book. But he was emphatic; he was not a writer.

Despite Terry's assertion that he couldn't write the book, I managed to persuade him to work with me on a collaborative effort. Re-invigorated, and further inspired to at last take the project forward to a writing stage, Terry and I met over a matter of months to sift, filter and 'weed' the archive of something like a dozen or more bulging lever-arch files (nothing was stored electronically) and to try to get to the real nitty-gritty of the matter. This was no easy task – not least because of Terry's impossible-to-decipher handwriting. Unhelpfully, many of the notes were penned by him. The challenge sometimes deepened when even Terry couldn't work it out!

Sadly, it wasn't long into the joint effort that Terry tragically died. However, I made a vow to carry on and get the story of *Lone Wolf* out there. This was not only for Terry and his family, but also for Richard Playne Stevens – his story crying out for the telling.

I can only hope that Terry would have approved of the result, although it would surely have been enhanced by his involvement to completion.

It is a matter of great sadness that we could not have completed this book together, my friend.

Andy Saunders
East Sussex
2019

ACKNOWLEDGEMENTS

I am indebted to many who have helped with this project along the way, and to those who also helped Terry when he embarked on his ambitious research project into Richard Playne Stevens so many years ago.

Into the latter category must surely fall very many hundreds of people. Most certainly, they include far too many to list. Sadly, and looking through Terry's archive, I know that most of them are no longer with us. Into this category, especially, fall the pilots and ground crew and Richard Stevens' immediate family. It was fortuitous that Terry began his research when he did, and that he was able to gather valuable information, documents and photographs before it was too late. Without that work, so much would have been lost forever and the world would never have known the remarkable truth of Richard Stevens' story.

Those who have helped me to pull all of this together are also legion, but in no particular order of merit I must especially single out Chris Goss, Andrew Thomas, Andy Long, Winston Ramsey, Simon Parry, Peter Cornwell, Martin Mace, Gerry Burke, Ed McManus, Richard Molloy, Ron Clarke and the late Steve Hall.

There are so many others who have also helped with advice, information, photographs and with various steers and clues. Again, they are too many to mention. However, it is a fact that primary sources were simply those assembled by Terry. I have tried to pull together the information he garnered and put it into some kind of logical and readable order. Under the circumstances, though, I must just say a 'thank you' to all those others who have helped, directly and indirectly, along the way.

I must also thank John Davies and his wonderful team at Grub Street Publishing. John has been very long suffering, patient and understanding over the protracted period it has taken to pull this work together. Initially, after John agreed to publish the work as a joint venture with Terry Thompson and myself, we were poleaxed by the untimely death of Terry. Having been bequeathed the R P Stevens archive by Terry, and then agreeing to take the project on without him, serious constraints on the author's time due to work commitments and family health problems further conspired to stymie all efforts to get the project off the ground. Sometimes, it felt as though the story was destined never to be told. But now, thanks to John and his team, the tale of the 'Lone Wolf' is finally out there!

Last, but by no means least as they say, I should thank those close to me. In that respect, I see from the file references on some of the documents produced for the book that quite a few were generated, across a number of years, by Robyn and Lewis Saunders. So, thank you Robyn and Lewis.

And finally, of course, my thanks to Sarah who has had to endure me being shut away for long hours in my office – sometimes working through the night – as I laboured to complete the manuscript and attempt to fathom out what Terry had written!

It has been a pleasure to have had such wholehearted support from so many people. Thank you all.

Prologue

On a bitterly cold morning in January 1942, Albert Shoebridge of Brentwood, Essex, picked up his morning newspaper and read that the RAF's greatest nightfighter pilot had been killed. He was Flight Lieutenant Richard Playne Stevens DSO DFC & Bar.

Albert's mind went back to a moonlit night just 12 months previously when he saw a German aircraft dive across the moon's bright disc and disappear into the darkness. He remembered looking over towards the far horizon and there, banking at tree-top height against the flames of a growing fire, was the silhouette of a Hurricane night-fighter as it circled what was the burning wreckage of a German Dornier 17 bomber.

On another moonlit night, this time during September 1916, a searchlight from Dartford was reaching up, stabbing and piercing the night as it searched for a German Zeppelin which droned threateningly up the Thames Estuary towards the capital, its target.

Brothers James and Richard Stevens were fast asleep in their cottage at Gravesend when their mother woke them, calling: "Boys! Quick! He's coming down on fire!" James later recalled how the two brothers rushed to the bedroom window of the cottage to watch as the sky was completely lit up by the fierce conflagration, and then how they all cheered as the airship finally split into two angry red balls of fire and fell to earth somewhere to the north of the river.

After what was the first successful nightfighter interception over British soil, an elat-ed and victorious Lieutenant William Leefe-Robinson brought his BE2C biplane back to land at Sutton's Farm airfield, and back to what was countrywide public adulation and, ultimately, a Victoria Cross.

From his bedroom window, Richard had witnessed the very first nightfighter success over Britain. As he watched the incandescent glow of the burning airship slowly disap-pear on the distant horizon, it was a scene he would always remember.

Twenty-five years later, another boy, John Pratley, was woken by his father who rushed into the young lad's bedroom near Wellesbourne, Warwickshire, shouting: "Come and see a German bomber on fire!" The entire family crowded to the windows, cheering as they heard machine-gun fire and watched the stricken bomber describe its flaming arc across the sky; a sky now entirely illuminated by the spectacle which culminated with the climax of an explosion and tremendous orange fireball on the horizon when the Heinkel hit the ground.

High above, and unseen to the Pratley family, Richard Playne Stevens banked his Hurricane around in an orbit above Wellesbourne and watched with grim fascination as the flames wickedly consumed yet another raider scattered on the ground below him.

As he did so, and as it did with each of his victims, Richard Stevens' memory inexorably flashed back to that September night in 1916.

Events had turned full circle.

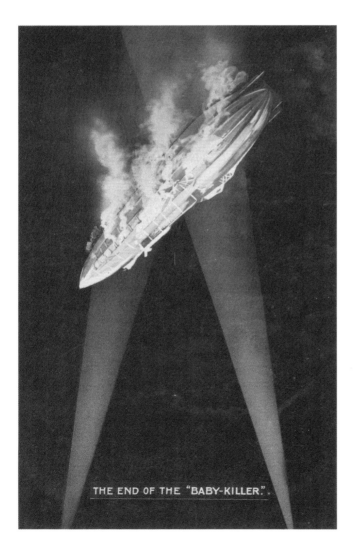

THE END OF THE "BABY-KILLER".

Depiction of the Zeppelin falling in flames at Cuffley that Richard and his brother James witnessed.

Chapter One

CHILDHOOD AND FAMILY LIFE

Richard Stevens was born into what would have been considered at that time an upper middle-class family on 11 September 1909 at the comfortable family home, 'Bankside' in Goldsmid Road, Tonbridge, Kent. Richard was the son of Sidney A Stevens and Isabel Dora Stevens (formerly Wilson) with Sidney's occupation described as coal factor, in which capacity he acted as broker between the coal suppliers and wholesalers and retailers. As to the family's status in the 'upper middle-class' bracket of society, they ultimately fell upon somewhat straitened circumstances just prior to the First World War when Sidney's business partner absconded with the assets, leaving Sidney to settle the company debts. House moves to apparently less salubrious dwellings would follow, including to a house in Gravesend during the war, before Sidney managed gradually to rebuild his life and his business. It was against this background, then, that Richard Stevens came into the world and into a life which would ultimately shape his future.

Richard Stevens, aged three-and-a-half. By the time of the 1911 census the name 'Playne' had been added.

One of seven children (six boys and a girl – James, Richard, Laurence, Robert, Tim, Phil and Helen), he is shown on his birth certificate and in all early official documentation as simply just Richard – albeit that he later became known as Richard Playne Stevens. It is certainly that name by which he is widely known, but it was not his given name at birth. According to Richard's elder brother James (upon whose recollection much of this examination of Richard's early life is based), the name Playne was a family surname on his mother's side. However,

Left: Richard's mother, Isabel, pictured with James at Christmas 1909.
Right: The three eldest brothers of the Stevens' clan; Richard (left), James (centre), and Laurence (right).

it is unclear when the name was added, or by whom. But it was certainly officially accepted as one of his forenames, even if it were a subsequent affectation on the part of Richard himself.

If constructing the detail of Richard's early life is challenging, and only possible through the testimony left by James Stevens, it is certainly clear that the family were somewhat bohemian in their approach to life and to living, and once they had settled back into more comfortable dwellings at Rusthall, Tunbridge Wells, in 1922 when Richard was 13, it was not uncommon for the family to go, en masse, on nocturnal hikes in the surrounding countryside. It was then, during these night-time jaunts, that it became clear to all that young Richard enjoyed one particularly exceptional physical attribute: excellent night vision. Such was his ability, in fact, that the party would deliberately get themselves 'lost' in the woods and countryside, intentionally taking no maps with them, and then allow Richard to lead them all home. Not only could he see things in the dark that the others could not see well, or at all, but he was also possessed of excellent spatial awareness and a comprehensively accurate mind-map of the local geography and topography. To the young Richard, it was nothing unusual. If anything, he was perplexed as to why others could not do the same as he. Nevertheless, it was with a marked degree of triumph that he would lead the entire family home, meandering through otherwise dark and featureless woods or fields, until the lamps of Rusthall village could be seen glimmering in the distance.

At home, Richard and his siblings led a happy and relatively carefree life. Theirs was not exactly a life of privilege or of plenty, but it was certainly one of contentment with what they had. Life for the Stevens family was relatively comfortable as compared to the lives of many ordinary folk of the period, although the children made much of the surrounding countryside which they loved, and which very much became their playground. There was also a sense of being free, in those kinder and gentler times, and they could more-or-less roam at will. Bows and arrows and simple adventures kept them amused, as did their shared love of nature and the great outdoors. Such things, such simple pleasures, were free and living on the edge of the Weald of Kent and Sussex was a great joy to all of them. As they got older, though, and their tastes evolved from bows and arrows and hide-and-seek in the countryside, the children all became excellent shots and were given Webley air pistols and rifles with which to practise their marksmanship. Richard's sister, Helen, recalled:

> "We were all very good at shooting. We used to hang old 78 records on the washing line and as they danced and turned in the wind, we used to shoot through the hole in the centre of the record with our Webley pistols. We were such good shots that if we missed and the records shattered into black shards onto the lawn, we would be horrified."

Three Firs at Rusthall, Tunbridge Wells, was the family home for much of Richard's childhood.

But the family idyll, like the records, would be shattered, piecemeal, as each sibling, in turn, was duly packed off to a variety of boarding schools. Notwithstanding the fact that the family were clearly still struggling to pull themselves back, financially, after the business catastrophe and massive economic impacts of the Great War, influenza pandemic and Great Depression of the late 1920s and 30s, all of the children were sent for private education. It seems, though, that all of them won scholarships to the various schools each attended. Even so, whether these were full scholarships which were fully funded or not, there would have invariably been some financial burden on the Stevens family. But it certainly seems to be the case that Sidney decided he wanted to keep the family in the manner to which he felt they should be accustomed. And in the case of young Richard, he was sent to the relatively prestigious Hurstpierpoint College in West Sussex, not too far from the family home.

Arriving there in the Christmas term of 1920, aged 11, Richard was assigned to Fleur de Lys House although his time at school there was not a particularly happy one. Neither academic nor particularly sporting, Richard features not at all in the record of any school achievements until his final two years there; in 1927 he played at three-quarters for his house side at rugby, although apparently without any particular distinction, and again for the school Second XV in 1928. However, there was one activity at Hurst-

Top: *The complete family pictured on holiday in the West Country in 1925. Bottom: The back garden at Rusthall, where Richard and his siblings would practise their marksmanship.*

pierpoint which was right up his street: shooting. In this capacity, he took part in school and inter-school competitions, including at Bisley, and would go on to win a shooting cap and was also granted his Certificate 'A' in the school's officer training corps. Notable in respect of his shooting at school, though, is this record of him in the school magazine, the *Hurst-Johnian*: "On his day, a good shot, but far too temperamental to be safe. He would do far better to control his temper when things go badly."

Telling remarks, indeed.

Otherwise, his time at school was entirely unremarkable although those who knew him then had some clear recall about Richard. All told, he was singularly 'ordinary' at school and might otherwise have been all but forgotten by his peers but for his emergence into the spotlight of fame in 1941. Then, with a Hurstpierpoint connection being made in the press, his contemporaries thought back to their school days and gave their recollections. Even at school, though, Richard had been a loner; a boy with no real friends, not even in his own house. One contemporary, George Twine, recalled:

> "I well remember him because he was much disliked by members of the Fleur de Lys. It was believed that he did not wash himself properly and was therefore dirty. He became 'Dirty Dick'. I do not think that he had any friends in the house. He was repeatedly ragged, and on one occasion he ran away from school for fear of being ragged. He was a quiet boy with few if any friends in the entire school."

Another contemporary, John Watts, only "dimly remembered" Richard Stevens:

> "He wasn't notable at all, although having thought about him I do recall that
> he had a rather piercing look in his eyes. Had we known what he would go on
> to achieve, I think we'd have taken far more notice of him!"

Only one other entry of any real note exists in the magazine of October 1928, record-ing that Richard Stevens had been awarded the drawing prize. Again, and apart from this recognition, there is otherwise no indication that Richard was particularly artistic, although a talent or penchant for painting rather surreal and slightly demonic imagery would emerge somewhat later. But, for 1928, it was the penultimate entry. The last comment being a single line, stating: "R P Stevens is going to Australia."

By the time Richard left school in the summer of 1928, he had little idea as to what it was that he wanted to do with his life. Certainly, he had no intention nor any aspi-ration to follow his father into the coal broker business. He was not, either, a young man suited for office work of any kind, and neither did he have any skill sets particu-larly to enable such skills to guide a career choice. Instead, he craved adventure, adored life outdoors and loved shooting. Little wonder, then, that the Australian Big Brother Movement of the day appealed to Richard and his spirit of adventure. And it would also solve the difficult problem of finding meaningful employment at the time of a national and international slump.

The Big Brother Movement owed its genesis to discussions between Australian and British business leaders at the 1923 Wembley exhibition; talks concerned with stim-ulating youth migration to Australia. Its basic idea was simple enough: each youth emigrating (the 'Little Brother') would be given an adult person in Australia (the 'Big Brother') who would provide encouragement, advice and support during the young mi-grant's early adjustment period in the new country. Its founder was Sir Richard Linton, a businessman and philanthropist.

Understandably, there was a natural reluctance by parents to permit migration of their sons so far from the British Isles when they were so young and so inexperienced. The 'Big Brother' provision was intended to respond to parents' fears, and the British agent for the movement in Australia, Bankes Amery, gave additional reasons for the founding of the Big Brother Movement when he wrote in 1926:

> "The basis of the Big Brother Movement was the establishment of a set of
> conditions that would attract a better class of boy to Australia; a boy who
> had been brought up in a better class of home and who had up till the mo-
> ment not been induced to leave Britain in any numbers... The boys whom
> the Big Brother Movement was out to cater for were the type who obtained

commissions during the war by promotion from the ranks... no previous scheme has been sufficiently attractive to middle-class parents."

The Little Brother was intended to be a physically fit, upright, clean-cut, well-mannered British young man who was determined to work hard on the land in Australia. His application to Australia House was to be accompanied by references as to ability and character from his school, a minister of his church and another leading citizen. He then had to pass the usual medical checks at Australia House and, if accepted, was granted an assisted passage to Australia. These conditions of joining, voluntarily accepted, enshrined middle-class virtues of sobriety, thrift and respect for the 'Little Brother's' social superiors and were intended to appeal to middle-class parents. In this respect, Sidney and Isabel supported the young Richard wholeheartedly in his venture. It would, they felt, be 'the making of him'.

Although we can be sure that Richard left for Australia in 1928, very little is known of his time there, who his 'Big Brother' was or where he worked – apart from the fact that it was on a cattle farm. Here, Richard learned to ride and had also taken with him from England a veritable arsenal of weaponry, including a .22 target pistol. Very often, he would carry around with him quite an armoury – the whole ensemble being complemented with a fearsome leather stock whip. His brother, James, recalled a story from Richard's outback days:

A passport photograph of Richard taken in October 1928. In preparation for his departure to Australia.

"He was especially keen on one particular girl, and he knew she went to church. One Sunday, he rode up to meet her as she came out of the service and he was, as usual, carrying his own personal arsenal. As his mount trotted up to the church, with the suave and well-armed Richard in the saddle, a group of local lads began to tease and heckle him, laughingly calling: 'Who do you think you are, Billy the Kid? It's all very well going around armed to the teeth, but you couldn't hit a haystack at five yards!' At that moment, a hapless rabbit hopped into sight about 20 paces away. Almost without looking, Richard unholstered his .22 pistol, aimed almost casually in the rabbit's direction and fired. Not only did he hit it, but he shot it cleanly through the head. Right between the eyes. They didn't make fun of him after that. But I don't know if it impressed the girl enough for her to either welcome or reciprocate Richard's attention!"

Exactly why the Australian dream turned sour for Richard, or didn't work out, remained unknown to his family and siblings, but during the depression many of the 'Big Brothers' were in financial difficulties and their 'Little Brothers' could not be further from their minds. As a result, and during the 1930s, some 350 'Little Brothers' returned to Britain. One of them was Richard.

The only known photograph of Richard in Australia as a farmer's boy, taken in July 1929.

Before moving on chronologically with the detail of Richard Stevens' life and career, it is necessary to look first at a most bizarre set of circumstances in the immediate run-up to war and which resulted in the death of one of his siblings.

With war looming, quite literally, the Stevens family were making their own collective and individual preparations for hostilities. At least, so far as any family could in these most uncertain of times. Richard, by now re-mustered as a sergeant pilot in the RAF Volunteer Reserve, was already focused on his chosen career path in aviation, albeit that this had now taken a military rather than a civilian route. His younger brother Robert Francis, however, had no fixed occupation in the weeks leading up to the war, although having previously served in the Artist's Rifles it is possible that the 27-year-old was considering re-enlistment with his old unit if hostilities began. Either way, he would not live to see the outbreak of war on 3 September 1939.

A keen amateur canoeist, and an experimental inventor, he had taken his canoe to a lonely stretch of the River Ouse at Barcombe Mills, near Lewes, East Sussex, during the first week of August 1939, but for reasons which remain shrouded in considerable mystery. All that we do know is that he was found dead on Friday 11 August, in his 12 ft canvas canoe and with his head having been almost completely shattered by an explosive charge. It was hardly a usual event for the local police or coroner to have to attend

Richard's brother Robert.

to, with the local *Kent & Sussex Courier* noting that: "… at first it appeared to contain all the elements of one of the most dramatic murder mysteries in recent years." Ultimately, and according to the authority of the day, it proved not to be a murder. Instead, it turned out to be an accident arising from the premature or unplanned explosion of a depth-charge weapon which Robert had been experimenting with. Accidental death through depth-charge experimentation was hardly on the radar of the East Sussex constabulary, either. However, the only available explanations for the event can be found in the detailed investigations of the police on behalf of HM Coroner, Dr E F Hoare; at least, to the extent that it was reported in the local and national newspapers of the day.

In the extensive newspaper reportage, it emerged that whilst Robert Stevens was unemployed, he was not in the least bothered by the fact that he was out of work and it was specifically stated that he "had money". Giving evidence, his father Sidney Stevens remarked that Robert was shortly to go on a trip to Spain and Portugal with "a number of other men", and although their identity was unknown to Sidney or anyone else, Robert Stevens would be receiving payment for this journey. It was also a journey, apparently, which was to be imminently made by canoe – paddling first across to Calais and then following the French coast all the way round to Spain and on to Portugal. By any standards, and especially given the prevailing and very uncertain European political situation, it was surely a somewhat strange undertaking. For that reason, then, and let alone because of the unusual circumstances of Robert's death, it is likely to be why officers of Special Branch became involved and "…were informed as to the full facts of the case".

In the evidence submitted to the Coroner's Court, it was revealed that Robert had constructed an experimental depth charge using a piece of steel pipe, using explosives and a shotgun cartridge detonator fixed to a wooden board. The whole Heath Robinson contraption was capable of being lowered to the riverbed by rope and, as the evidence unfolded in court, it became clear that Robert had been in his canoe and had lowered the device into the water. When it had failed to detonate, it is thought that he had retrieved it and was examining it "while still strapped in his canoe" when the device exploded. Adding to the mystery was the fact that the incident had occurred at midnight, and that Superintendent Holloway of Lewes Police later reported that a man (whose name the police declined to disclose) had since taken Holloway to the scene of the incident. This, it was reported, had "…altered the whole line of inquiry". It also seems to have been something which triggered the involvement of Special Branch.

The whole episode seems as surreal as it is bizarre. As one newspaper report put it, "the mystery was not solved" by the inquest, even although the coroner's jury returned a unanimous verdict on Robert Francis Stevens of 'Accidental Death' at Forester's Hall, Lewes, on 29 August 1939. We do not know how, if at all, Richard Stevens was affected by his brother's death. However, by the time of Robert's funeral, war had already been declared and Richard does not seem to have attended the ceremony to say his farewells to his sibling.

It remains a puzzling episode involving a family who, to put it bluntly, did not exactly conform to the norms of society at that time. Individually, if not collectively, family members might reasonably be described as oddly eccentric. And that would not be an unfair description with which to tag Richard, who returned to the family fold with a marked degree of eccentricity and showmanship.

SHOT WITH HOME-MADE GUN

CANOEIST'S DEATH FOUND TO BE ACCIDENTAL

The death of ROBERT FRANCIS STEVENS, aged 27, of Frant Road, Tunbridge Wells, whose body was found fixed in an overturned canoe in the River Ouse at Rodmell, near Lewes, on August 11, with a gunshot wound in the head, was accidental. This was the verdict of the jury at the inquest on his body at Lewes yesterday.

It was pointed out that murder was originally suspected, but the CORONER, Dr. E. F. Hoare, ruled it out as inconceivable. Stevens was shot with a home-made contrivance consisting of a length of piping.

Arthur Rollison, of Meeching Road, Newhaven, who said he had been fishing with Stevens, said that Stevens had constructed a centre-board to his canoe of his own design, and it was filled with beach and gravel to assist him in bad weather. He was very cheerful and without apparently a care in the world.

Mrs. A. Jacobs, of Southborough, said that Stevens picked up a piece of pipe in her garden and said he wanted to make a depth charge with it. He was of an inventive nature.

Stevens's friend, Edward Jacobs, of Faversham, said that a 12-bore cartridge found on Stevens was similar to some in the witness's possession. Stevens had spoken of making a cannon from tubing.

Police-constable Whitewood said that dragging operations brought up, 2ft. from the canoe, a piece of piping about 5in. long to which was tied a piece of rope about 12ft. long. The piping had a bent nail at one end, and was later found to be an improvized weapon.

Allen Edwards, a gunsmith, said that if the weapon were exploded under water one would expect a piece of cord to be attached to it for its recovery. Unless handled with great care the weapon might cause an accident.

The CORONER said that the "Heath Robinson" weapon was just the sort of thing that might be used as an experimental depth charge. A verdict of accidental death was returned.

A newspaper report covering the story of Robert's death.

Chapter Two

PALESTINE AND FLYING

Although the family had been aware of Richard's impending return to Tunbridge Wells, his arrival back at the family home one spring morning in 1932 took them all completely by surprise as they awoke to what sounded like pistol shots. Venturing downstairs to investigate, sister Helen saw a figure silhouetted in the open doorway to the garden – it was a figure brandishing a fearsome leather bull whip and wearing an Australian bush hat, looking for all the world like a much earlier incarnation of Indiana Jones. As he stood there, the crack, crack, crack of the whip sounded like the report of pistol shots. Each crack, though, saw another daisy head deftly removed from the lawn. Delighted by the return of her very own 'Big Brother', Helen excitedly indicated specific daisies on the lawn which she wanted Richard to decapitate. With a flick of the wrist, and the sharp 'snap' of the whip, the specific daisy heads would be sent spiralling through the air, much to Helen's delight.

Now home again, Richard was again at a loose end and needed to find some form of gainful employment. And there was precious little of it to be had. Once more, Richard began to think of something overseas and he then spotted a recruiting advert to join the British Palestine Police and he was immediately sold on the idea. Not only did it offer adventure, but also secure and steady employment and good pay and conditions.

The Palestine Police Force was a British colonial police service established in Mandatory Palestine on 1 July 1920, when High Commissioner Herbert Samuel's civil administration took over responsibility for security from General Allenby's Occupied Enemy Territory Administration (South).

The Egyptian Expeditionary Force won the decisive Battle of Gaza in November 1917 under General Allenby who accepted the surrender of Jerusalem. The city was placed under martial law and guards were posted in Jerusalem and Bethlehem to protect sites held sacred by the Christian, Muslim and Jewish religions. Then, following a decisive British victory at the Battle of Megiddo, the Ottoman Empire formally surrendered on 30 October 1918, leaving the British in complete control of Palestine.

Initially, Palestine was administered in the southern district of the Occupied Enemy Territory Administration (OETA) and the Palestine Police Force was founded with the establishment in July 1920 of the civilian administration of the British Mandate.

The police force at the time consisted of 18 British officers supported by 55 Palestinian officers and 1,144 rank and file, whose duties were described as:

> "Besides fulfilling the ordinary duties of a constabulary, such as the preservation of law and order and the prevention and detection of crime, they shall act as their numbers will allow as escorts for the protection of tax collectors, serve summonses issued by the judicial authorities, distribute government notices and escort government treasure throughout the country."

It was into this organisation, then, that Richard enlisted not long after his return from Australia, but having left no letters or records of his time with the Palestine Police we can only rely on Richard's brother, James, to fill us in with a little hearsay detail of his time with the force. It was a time which was unsurprisingly filled with unrest and rioting as the Palestine Police attempted with varying degrees of success to keep apart the Muslims, Christian Arabs, Druze, Armenians, Egyptian Copts and the urbanites and fellaheen and to maintain some semblance of law and order. Then, as now, the region was a boiling cauldron of anger, resentment and tribal and religious confrontation. For Richard, his time there saw him develop a fellow feeling for those he saw as the underdogs – particularly the Arabs. As he studied and became enmeshed in the chaotic world of the Middle East, so he became fascinated with the history

Top: Constable Richard Playne Stevens of the Palestine Police Force, c.1931. Bottom: T E Lawrence, or Lawrence of Arabia. Richard's obsession with Lawrence remained right up until his death.

Richard, right, relaxing in off-duty hours with other officers of the Palestine Police Force. From left to right: Const. Burgess, Cpl Fackrel, Cpl Rayner, Const. Smith and Richard Stevens.

which had led to the world in which he had now become immersed. Unsurprisingly, he became fascinated by the works of Lawrence of Arabia and Lawrence's writings. In fact, it was an interest which became more than somewhat obsessive, and during his tenure in Palestine, Richard's favourite book – his joy and his travelling companion, in fact – was Lawrence's *Revolt in the Desert*. Given the work on which Richard was then engaged, it was a singularly appropriate title.

Quite what happened to end Richard's career with the Palestine Police Force is unclear, but it certainly seems to be the case that he had a clash with his superiors. Given his dislike of authority, and that anything he perceived as injustice was anathema to Richard, it must certainly have appeared that, at times, he was enforcing British administered law against sections of the local populace and sometimes felt there to be unfairness and discrimination. His hero, Lawrence, was 'his own man' and Richard began to increasingly feel that way, too. And in the disciplined ranks of a colonial police force that surely wasn't going to end well. James recalls one story from that period:

> "Riots involving one element or other of the local population were common-
> place, and at around the time of Dick's service the Palestine Police Force had
> introduced a dog section. Now, I cannot say whether Richard was part of that
> section or not, but he had certainly managed to 'acquire' one of the section's
> dogs. It was a massive and mean-tempered Rhodesian Ridgeback, and when
> Dick's section had received intelligence that there would be some kind of riot

or disturbance the following day he let it be known that he would be bringing a lion in to quell the disorder should any trouble arise. And he made sure that the threat was fed to the right people. It was a threat, though, met with some derision. But the threat must have registered, all the same.

"Now, this dog was sort of lion coloured, and the physical side profile of the breed is quite 'lion-esque'. So, to follow through on the threat, Dick created a 'mane' of string or wool and attached it around the dog's collar. Then, as the public disorder began to build, so Dick drove slowly towards the throng of advancing people with the dog riding on the bonnet of his truck, the hound pacing this way and that, at the end of a long chain. Suddenly, the rioters stopped in their tracks and, as Dick made to unchain the 'lion', so the rioters turned and fled. It was just the sort of hare-brained scheme that Dick would have dreamed up. But it worked!"

In all probability, the powers that be would not have disapproved of the somewhat unconventional method adopted by Richard Stevens to stop this instance of disorder. But his unconventional methods would ultimately lead him into hot water. One of the things which Richard had taken with him to Palestine was his Australian bull whip, and on one occasion he took it with him to confront the rioters. And it seemingly ended his career – at least, with the uniformed force. James, again:

"The story came to me that he had an order to go out and quell yet another riot and they were told to go unarmed. Not even with truncheons. He and his colleagues regarded this as bloody ridiculous, and so Dick took his bull whip with him. They were certainly expecting trouble. However, a couple of cracks of the whip and the riot ceased. I can imagine, in fact, that he probably nipped a piece out of somebody's bum with it. Or left a rioter or two with some stinging wheals. But I don't know that. Anyway, Dick was on the carpet the next morning and he was fired on the spot."

The aftermath, though, seems not to have been an absolute dismissal from the Palestine Police per se, but

'Paddy' the Rhodesian Ridgeback. The caption to the reverse of the original photograph reads: "One of these will give a lion a lot to think about."

The somewhat surreal paintings on the wall of this Palestine Police Force bar and lounge were painted by Richard Stevens. The aeroplane monster, top right, is noteworthy – as is the general style of artwork, a style which would re-emerge much later when Richard painted a dramatic emblem on his nightfighter Hurricane.

rather a removal from the front-line branch. James Stevens explains:

> "Immediately he was fired, somebody else recruited him for what I believe was the narcotics squad – or something to do with anti-smuggling operations – although I'm not absolutely sure if that was with the police or with the customs service out there. The thing is, Dick was far too hot headed and unpredictable to be dealing with rioting Arabs or Jews. It needed somebody who was calm and unexcitable for that job, and Dick was neither of those things! Anyway, I think he only lasted a very short while in his new post. It probably wasn't exciting enough for him and during the mid-1930s he came home. I seem to think it was officially for a spell of home leave, or maybe he'd resigned. I just can't remember. But he never went back."

In fact, even if he were contemplating a return to Palestine, a chance meeting while at home in Kent would certainly change the entire direction of Richard Stevens' life. And it was into the oddly eccentric world of Richard, and the Stevens clan generally, that a young lady named Mabel Hyde was ultimately drawn. Again, brother James recalled:

"I was going about with this girl Irah at the time, and every so often a whole gang of us would have a bit of a party at The Old Barn, Hildenborough, which was just on the outskirts of Tonbridge. Now and again, it fell to me to make the party plans and it would involve anything from 12 to 24 people. I think we paid five bob a head or something, but if we wanted eggs and bacon in the early hours it would be a little bit more. Anyway, on this occasion, it was when Dick had come home from Palestine and so I got Irah to invite her sister, Mabel, and Dick came too. Well, that was that. Before very long they were together, and I don't know if it was because of meeting her or not, but he didn't go back to Palestine after they hooked up together."

It wasn't long after this that Richard and Mabel (actually Olive Mabel) became engaged to be married, before eventually marrying on 24 August 1935 at St Paul's Church in Rusthall, Tunbridge Wells, and with the couple then settling into a property at Shermanbury in West Sussex, just a few miles to the north of Shoreham-by-Sea and the busy airport nestling alongside the River Adur, under the South Downs.

While it remains something of a mystery as to what Richard's source of income was at this time, his brother describes him as being "at a loose end" and, according to James, he decided to enrol with the Civil Air Guard in order "to learn to fly". That, however, is not exactly borne out by other information, most notably the Royal Aero Club's record relating to the granting of his aviator's certificate.

Top: A fairly suave-looking Richard in the garden of his Palestine Police quarters before heading back to England in 1932. Bottom: Inscribed: "To Grannie with love from Dick, 1932", Richard still looks very boyish in this photograph. The next eight or nine years would see him 'age' considerably.

Richard and Mabel on their wedding day, 24 August 1935, at Rusthall, Tunbridge Wells.

According to the Royal Aero Club's records, Richard was granted his Flying Licence on 8 August 1936, at Redhill Flying Club on a DH60 Moth. At this date, Richard is shown as still residing with his parents at 'Three Firs', Rusthall, Kent. The date of granting the licence, however, pre-dates by two years the founding of the Civil Air Guard in 1938, an organisation which was established to provide service pilots who could assist the RAF in times of emergency. So, unless Richard had joined the Civil Air Guard in another capacity and at some later date, it would appear he didn't do so with a view to learning to fly. Thus, in this respect, James' recollection is incorrect – although he was adamant that it was Richard's wife, Mabel, who had funded his flying lessons. Additionally, Richard had also enlisted in the RAF Volunteer Reserve (RAFVR) in July 1937, at which time he was shown as Aircraftsman 2nd Class, Under Training Pilot. One other mystery, too, surrounds the identity of the instructor who taught him to fly.

Family legend very forcefully has it that his instructor was Cecil Lawrence Pashley, almost the founding father of Shoreham Airport and proprietor of the South Coast Flying Club. That Richard might have learned to fly with him – or at least taken some lessons at Shoreham or been a member of the flying club – makes perfect sense. First, Shoreham was only just a few miles distant from the marital home (which in 1937 was at Upper Brighton Road, Lancing), although Redhill was slightly closer to Tunbridge Wells where Richard was probably living when he started his flying training. Additionally, and of greater significance, Cecil Pashley was apparently a cousin of Lawrence of Arabia. It begs the question, therefore: would Richard have been likely to pass up an opportunity to learn to fly with his hero's cousin, or to have missed out on being a member of his flying club?

However, we do know that Richard flew from Shoreham at the time Cecil Pashley was

STEVENS. Richard P.   **14170**

                    Three Firs,
                        Rusthall,
                            Tunbridge Wells,
Born 11th Sept. 1909.   *at* Tonbridge.   Kent.
Nationality   British.
Rank, Regiment, Profession
Certificate taken on   D.H. 60. Gipsy 1. 85.
At   Redhill Flying Club.
Date 8.8.36.

The Royal Aeronautical Society's record of Richard gaining his flying certificate.

active there as his friend, Rita Spinney, recalled:

> "Dick Stevens and I were in a circle of friends in the Shoreham area – all part
> of a fairly bohemian group – which included some real characters such as
> Tommy Farr the famous Lonsdale Belt boxer. There were a number of slightly
> raffish drinking and dancing clubs that were set up in old railway carriages
> by the River Adur. One was 'Flo's', run by a woman called Florrie Ford, and
> 'The Riverside Club' run by the Houston sisters, Rene and Winifred. They
> were cabaret clubs, really, and Dick was part of that set although he was of-
> ten morose, moody and surly. He came to the club alone, and I never realised
> that he was married until very much later. He never seemed short of cash
> and one summer night in 1936, he called for me at my home and walked me
> to the airport as he'd invited me for a flight. He got me in the seat and put
> my headgear on and we took off for a flight over the sea and back over the
> countryside behind the airport. It was about a half-hour flight. I was really
> very excited because it was the very first time I'd flown. When we landed, he
> told me that I was the first passenger he'd taken up after having only very re-
> cently passing his test. Anyway, we walked to the bar in the airport building
> to get a celebratory drink. He said that he wanted to celebrate that he'd got
> us up and back down again in one piece. And there was I thinking that Dick
> was an experienced pilot and knew what he was doing!"

However, the exact route Richard Stevens took formally to get into aviation is a little
uncertain, and none of his flying logbooks have survived to help unravel the story. And
neither do we know, exactly, how he then progressed through professional development into commercial aviation. However, it was Frank Griffith, the proprietor of the
Croydon-based Air Couriers Ltd. who gave him a job during March 1938, and who later
wrote of Stevens:

> "My association with him went back some years before the war when he was
> making a difficult start in aviation and I was able to fix him up with, I think,
> his first job in flying. This was after he had had a bit of a mishap with his
> aircraft and damaged another on the ground in 1937. He was a charming
> but slightly eccentric man who modelled himself on Lawrence of Arabia, and
> occasionally he would appear for work wearing Arab headdress!"

Work with Air Couriers Ltd. was varied, if not a little sporadic. However, for the day,
Richard Stevens would earn good money with the company, although his letter offering engagement with them from Frank Griffith proposed the princely sum of a £4 per
week retainer, and with hourly flying pay to be set at 5/- (day flying) and 15/- (night

flying). Richard was having none of it and wrote back to say that he wanted £5 per week as a retainer and 10/- per hour daytime flying pay. Seemingly, Frank Griffith agreed, and Richard Stevens commenced work with the company at the beginning of April 1938. However, it was employment which only came about as a result of Richard having to cancel a trip to India "...because of the Austrian business" which he mentioned in correspondence with Griffith. The 'Austrian business', of course, was the German Anschluss of Austria which was then causing regional instability and uncertainty throughout Europe. Quite likely, it also put a block on Richard's departure given his status with the RAFVR at that time. Or, at the very least, Richard felt he could not travel overseas at a time of international crisis in the event that he should be called up for RAFVR service.

Despite what is otherwise a complete paucity of detail regarding his civilian flying career, from paperwork preserved by Frank Griffith we can at least deduce that the aircraft regularly flown by Richard Stevens was a DH80 Puss Moth, G-ABLB. The aircraft was primarily used for the role of army co-operation flying. However, Richard's first flying assignment was with Frank Griffith in a DH89 Dragon Rapide for a night army co-operation flight in order that Stevens could: "...get the hang of the geography of London by night."

As it would turn out, extensive night flying over the home counties would, in some respects, later stand Richard Stevens in good stead. But it would also be a two-edged sword. As he built up night-flying hours, and with increasing work on army co-operation flights, it would ultimately propel him, much to his chagrin, into RAF army anti-aircraft co-operation units when war finally broke out. As Frank Griffith recalled: "In the event, he proved to be an excellent and hard-working pilot and with us he built up his experience largely in flying night-time army co-operation flights for searchlight training."

And it was on this type of flying, on contract work for the Air Ministry and War Office, that Richard Stevens spent much of his time when flying for Air Couriers Ltd. At the time, 'Jimmy' Jenkins was a ground engineer with the company at Croydon and sometimes flew with the pilot he just knew as 'Steve':

> "Most of the pilots were hired on a casual basis when the weather was suitable. We were very busy, flying mostly in the evenings up until midnight when all the aircraft were then returned to Croydon for overnight re-fuelling, daily inspections and to be readied for the early morning newspaper runs to France, on which 'Steve' often flew. I cannot ever recall using 'Steve's' real name, but he was very popular. He had no side to him as many of the jumped-up 'drivers' did. Anyway, the ground crew were allowed to fly with the aircraft if there was little to do on the ground, and I flew with 'Steve' whenever I could. On one occasion, it was a daylight patrol for the army,

somewhere north of London I believe, and they were tracking us with their sound locators.

"We were in Monospar G-ABDN which was a specially made aircraft with a Gypsy Major engine and had an amazing rate of climb and a very useful cruising speed. As the flying was very boring, I took along some *Picture Post* and other magazines to read and we had settled down to fly the circuit and had picked all the turning points. We were flying at about 5,000 feet, so I started reading – or ogling the girlie models in the magazines. 'Steve' couldn't see the pictures clearly enough. So, he swung the control column over to me and grabbed the magazines and said: 'You have control.' I'd never flown an aircraft before, and he just muttered: 'Keep it on course, keep it level on the artificial horizon and keep the same altitude and airspeed.' Coming up to turning points, I vaguely remembered that it was advisable to drop the nose slightly so that it wouldn't stall. This actually resulted in the nose dropping very rapidly, whereupon 'Steve' quickly grabbed the controls, showed me how to turn correctly and then went back to the magazine! I realised from this that flying was just 'a piece of cake' and ultimately, from 'Steve's' influence, I went on to become a pilot myself."

'Jimmy' went on to add:

"I don't think that 'Steve' was ever adjudged a better night pilot than any of the others we had, and he was junior to many other pilots, and he was way less experienced, really. However, to my way of thinking, 'Steve's' ability at night stemmed from the endless round of night flying on army co-operation, working with the searchlights, and doing the newspaper runs to France. He was doing it time and again, over and over."

Certainly, and elements of danger notwithstanding, the work with Air Couriers was also earning him good money with his pay, for example, on 15 July 1938 totalling £17- 5/- for the week. It was a healthy wage, and with Mabel now pregnant, the pair moved into a house called 'Caerhayes' in Shirley Hill Road, Croydon, but with Richard now having an eye to career progression. This was no doubt prompted by the birth, on 18 December 1938, of twins Frances Marie and John Lawrence (after Lawrence of Arabia) to Richard and Mabel. Now, family responsibilities meant a more pressing need to ensure the financial welfare of the new family unit.

Croydon, a bustling and growing airport, was home to increasing numbers of smaller 'airlines', or, rather, operators of short-haul passenger and freight aircraft. One such was Wrightways, a small airline formed by the partnership of R V Wrightson and G P McGivney and operating a miscellany of aircraft types such as the DH86, DH89, DH84

The Stevens twins, John Lawrence (left) and Frances Marie – the latter becoming the very apple of Richard's eye.

Dragon, and DH80 Puss Moth – but offering a regular position rather than the ad hoc and almost part-time role with Air Couriers. Exactly when he joined Wrightways is unrecorded, but his last pay cheque from Air Couriers was issued on 3 February 1939, and so we might reasonably assume it to have been shortly thereafter.[1]

When Richard Stevens arrived at Wrightways, Guy Ashenden was a radio officer who often flew with Stevens, and, as far as he was concerned, he already had 'Cat's Eyes' capabilities – and this was long before the newspapers would bestow that sobriquet in wartime.

> "I flew with 'Steve' on the DH86. It was said that at the time, and if you wanted to find a really thick fog, all you had to do was go to Croydon Airport. I can definitely confirm that his night sight was pretty nigh on incredible, for not only did he have the ability to see in the fog and the mist, but he also had this natural instinct of a homing pigeon. Despite the fact that Croydon was lit with a 750,000 candle-power neon beacon, floodlights, and with the buildings all picked out in red lights, these all became invisible in fogs or smogs. But not to 'Steve'."

Despite the weather problems, incessant night flying and limitations (sometimes) of both aircraft and pilots, there were precious few accidents. However, 'Jimmy' Jenkins thought this was down to a fair degree of luck, especially given the sheer weight of the newspapers being flown out to France: "Newspapers were very heavy, and I'm sure most aircraft took off well above the maximum all-up weight."

Nevertheless, and although not cargo related, just flying the army co-operation flights was not without risk, either. On the evening of 25 April 1938, for instance, Wrightways lost DH Dragon G-ACHX at Croydon at 21.30 hours after a co-op flight. The aircraft circled Croydon, prepared to land, and then crashed into trees beyond the south-western boundary when the starboard engine failed. The pilot, 25-year-old Colin Byer, died in hospital a short time afterwards. Luckier was his wireless operator,

---

1   Rather confusingly, details recorded on Richard's RAF Record of Service show: 'Commercial Pilot N.E Airways 1938 – 1939 and Commercial Pilot Wrightways 1939 – 1940'.

Ernest Ratcliffe, although Ratcliffe was quite severely injured. Although this incident pre-dated Richard Stevens' eventual engagement with Wrightways, he was working at Croydon Airport with Air Couriers and he knew Colin Byer, the first fatality in his circle of aviation friends. It illustrated only too painfully to him that, however good the pilot, aviation could be deadly when things went wrong.

Also working at Wrightways when Richard Stevens joined was an old colleague from Air Couriers, 'Jimmy' Jenkins, who would go on to enjoy yet more flights with 'Steve'. One, though, was rather more memorable than it was enjoyable:

"We were flying in DH86, G-AEJM, when I decided to go to the back of the cabin to enjoy one of the fruits of modern aeroplane development: an Elsan toilet! On the way back to the cockpit, 'Steve' mischievously put the nose down violently, then pulled up with the same force. The result was that I was suspended, weightless, between the cockpit roof and the floor. I had the good sense to break my fall by grabbing some of the seat back rests, else I might have gone crashing out through the Sitka Spruce floorboards. It was very scary, but 'Steve' laughed all the way back to Croydon!"

An advertising leaflet for Wrightways, with whom Richard flew from Croydon Airport in the late 1930s.

Not a laughing matter, though, was the inexorable march towards hostilities. As darkening war clouds gathered over Europe, so the army co-operation flying undertaken by Wrightways increased in its frequency and tempo. Exponentially, so did Richard Stevens' flying hours.

As the summer of 1939 began to fade towards autumn, it became apparent that war was all but inevitable. With that inevitability, however, tangible and worrying indicators began to manifest themselves. At Croydon Airport, RAF aircraft sometimes landed and departed. Now, none of them carried the overall silver schemes with bright squadron markings. Now, they were painted in drab camouflage and even the airport buildings, including the massive terminal, were draped in camouflage netting as ARP centres and sandbagged shelters sprang up, windows had sticking tape applied against blast and the entire civilian population was being fitted out with gas masks. Along with generally increased military activity, they were chilling portents of what was to come. Watching events unfold and reasoning that Croydon Airport would become a

prime target (it was bombed heavily on 15 August 1940), Richard evacuated his family back to Sussex, renting No 2 Oaklands Farm Cottages, Shermanbury, in West Sussex. Here, he considered his family to be safe. Mabel was also closer to her relatives, including an aunt in Ditchling.

Finally, the inevitably of conflict was realised at the declaration of war on 3 September 1939, with all civilian aircraft being immediately placed under the control of the Air Ministry for RAF or official use. In the case of Wrightways, its aircraft, pilots and engineers were evacuated from Croydon and moved, en masse, to Barton Airport to continue contract flying on behalf of the military. Pilots like Richard Stevens, a RAFVR sergeant pilot, continued to fly the aircraft on very much the same basis as before, except in a different location. However, the period between September 1939 and the following spring was an uncertain one for Wrightways and the company's employees. Albert Archer, an engine mechanic, recalled:

Top: The G-AEJM, of Wrightways, which Richard sometimes flew. Bottom: From boy to man. Richard Stevens the airline pilot, c.1938. According to David Masters in So Few *(Eyre and Spottiswoode, 1941), Richard had achieved some 400 night-flying hours before the war, much of it on nocturnal newspaper delivery flights from Croydon to Paris.*

"We were not at Barton very long before all our aircraft were formally taken over by the RAF. The last one to go was a G-AFEZ, which we had bought brand new from de Havilland just before the war. With no aircraft, Wrightways then concentrated on engine overhaul work, almost exclusively Gipsy engines, but I do distinctly recall a special visit in 1941 from Richard Stevens when he arrived to see us in his all-black Hurricane with an impressive row of swastikas painted under the cockpit rail. There was a huge feeling of pride within the company that he was 'one of us'."

RAF Croydon on 15 August 1940 draws a crowd of spectators to witness the drama.

To many, including those who had worked with him at Wrightways, there was also a feeling that Richard Stevens was 'a bit too old' to ever be the fighter pilot he had so hankered to be. A feeling, too, that he might be much better suited to ferrying aircraft around for the Air Transport Auxiliary than a pilot in any capacity with the RAF – let alone flying with Fighter Command! Ultimately, sheer and dogged determination would see him achieve that goal.

Back at Shermanbury, Mabel had settled in with twins Frances and John to sit out the duration of the war. Meanwhile, Richard, based miles away near Manchester, was an infrequent visitor to the family home. In part, this was due to travel distances and the exigences of service life, although every time he could get petrol he would drive to Sussex in his Ford 10 until it finally broke down – a vehicle which those close to him strongly suspected to have been powered by high octane Air Ministry aviation spirit; a suspicion which gained further credibility when the car's engine exhaust valves finally burned out! But, according to Richard's brother, James, there was another reason for Richard's infrequent visits. The marriage was already under some strain, if not already on the rocks. As James put it:

> "It wasn't exactly a secret that the marriage had its problems. In fact, when they got together, we were surprised. Surprised that they hit it off. We simply thought that Richard was a confirmed bachelor and that he would remain so. He appeared to be a solid sort of person, and in general he was. But he had this ability to go into top revs and excitable overdrive simultaneously. He must have been an impossible man to live with, frankly."

The last pay cheque of £14 – 12 -/ for Richard from Air Couriers in September 1938 indicated a reasonable earning level for the time.

Now, though, enforced separation and service life exacerbated the cracks that had appeared in the relationship, such that when Richard could get home it was essentially just to see the children. Frances, especially attached to her father, would invariably greet him on the path to the cottage door grasping a bunch of wilting flowers she had helped to pick in anticipation of her father's return. She was the apple of his eye, and whenever he had to leave, she would be in floods of tears and completely inconsolable.

Across the winter of 1939 and 1940, and into the spring, an air of uncertainty pervaded all aspects of life in Britain. And so was there uncertainty, too, in the lives of Mabel and Richard. Mabel muddled on as best she could, alone with the twins, while Richard finally found himself posted away from Wrightways on 10 April 1940 to an RAF establishment: 110 Anti-Aircraft Co-operation Wing at nearby Ringway. As well as the personnel being transferred out to 110 Wing, so too were all the Wrightways aircraft, with most shown as also being transferred around 10 and 14 April to the RAF; largely, this was to 6 Anti-Aircraft Co-operation Unit (AACU) where they were also allocated RAF serial numbers to replace the civil registrations.

For Richard, it was just more of the same: more anti-aircraft co-operation flying in the very same aircraft. Now, though, the bright silver colour schemes of the Wrightways aircraft, with their smart chrome yellow cheat lines and black-edged registration lettering, had – for the most part – been replaced with camouflage paint, roundels and RAF serial numbers. And the stylish dark blue civilian airline uniform, with its braid, gold embroidered pilot's 'wings' and silver buttons, had been replaced with a drab RAF sergeant pilot's uniform.

Richard was at least still flying. But this wasn't what he wanted. He was restless. And he wanted to get into the war. Properly into the war.

Chapter Three

SERVICE PILOT AND FAMILY TRAGEDY

The only thing which had really changed on 10 April 1940, when Richard Stevens was posted to 110 Anti-Aircraft Wing, was that he was now officially flying on full-time service with the RAF. All else stayed the same; the same aircraft and same boring repetitive work flying up and down, round and round, to exercise anti-aircraft units, searchlights and sound locators. As a fellow airman at Ringway put it:

> "It was not exactly the most glamorous of occupations for a RAF pilot at that time. It became even less so when news of the Battle for France, Dunkirk and the Norway expedition hit the headlines with details of the air battles and our successes. By the time of the Battle of Britain, everyone wanted to be a fighter pilot."

All of these things frustrated Richard to the point of anger. He was, he felt, being wasted in such a backwater, however important a role the anti-aircraft co-operation units were playing. It was something that all who knew him at Ringway recalled; his constant badgering of authority to get moved to fighters, and incessantly bemoaning what he saw as his intolerable situation if anyone would care to listen to him in the sergeants' mess. It was something Arthur Markland, a colleague on the same unit, clearly recalled:

> "Stevens was not one to sit back and take it and he constantly bombarded the authorities with requests to be transferred to active flying duties; in particular, to fighters. In the sergeant's mess he was always going on about it and telling us what he would do if only they would give him the chance. Most of us just smiled and nodded our heads, humoring him, because I don't think any of us gave him a chance in hell of getting on to fighters owing to his age. After all, the average age of a fighter pilot was 22 and it was the service in which youth reigned supreme. Admittedly, there were many fighter pilots approaching their late twenties, but these were all men who had been constantly flying fighter aircraft for a number of years and who were now experienced flight commanders or pilots who had been promoted to lead squadrons through

seniority. How-
ever, if Sergeant
Stevens pos-
sessed one as-
set then it was a
great determina-
tion to persist in
his goal and not
to accept refusal
on any count."

Short Scion, G-ADDX, was one of the varied aircraft flown by Richard during his time with 6 AACU at Ringway.

Relentlessly, he pur-
sued that goal. Equally
relentlessly, he flew in
the same rag-tag collection of aircraft from the eclectic selection of impressed civilian
machines which made up the complement of the unit. Then, in June 1940, came a
brief moment of anticipation when he was notified that he would be posted. Against
a background of all that had been going on across the English Channel, was this his
moment? Was this his transfer for training prior to posting out to a fighter unit? Crest-
fallen, Richard read his posting orders which simply assigned him to 6 Anti-Aircraft
Co-Operation Unit at Ringway. Essentially, it wasn't a posting. Just the same old thing
in the same old place.

Wireless Operator Jack Walsh also found himself posted to 6 AACU from early June
1940, where he immediately found himself crewed up with a morose and taciturn pilot:
Sergeant Richard Stevens. It was with Richard that he made his first flight on the unit
on 3 June in a Percival Q6, G-ADMT, flying at various heights to exercise the Liverpool
guns. The next day, also with Richard, it was in a Short Scion, G-ADDX, to carry out
practice dive-bombing and low-level attacks at Oswestry – the monotony broken by:
'Lunch at RAF Shawbury' as recorded in Walsh's logbook. Here, in a different sergeant's
mess, Stevens sought out other unsuspecting sergeant pilots who might listen to his
angst as he railed against the stupidity of the powers that be for obstructing his progression onto fighters. Walsh, meanwhile, had spotted another wireless operator and
deliberately engaged him in small talk at another table to avoid his own embarrassment at the other sergeants' barely concealed derision of Stevens. He was, after all, a
man who was almost getting too old to be flying anything – let alone fighters!

Throughout the rest of June, and through to September, the flying routine continued much the same, although it was getting spiced up just a little by the inclusion of
military aircraft like the Fairey Battle, with Stevens piloting L5206 and L5209 on 17
June and 2 August. However, the knowledge that the Battle of Britain was now raging – particularly across southern England – just added to Richard's ire. Nevertheless,

and whatever his relationship was currently with Mabel, he at least was content in the knowledge that he had got his family to safety and out of Croydon. 'Safety', though, was a relative term when it came to life in any part of southern Britain during the high summer of 1940.

Called to the orderly office at Ringway one August day to take a telephone call, Richard found a distressed Mabel on the line: "They machine-gunned us at the Laine, Dick!", was all that he could hear. When he had calmed down, and once he knew that everyone was safe and unharmed, the red mist properly descended. "The bastards! Animals!", Stevens shouted to an increasingly alarmed audience in the office as he vented his violent yet impotent anger at the Luftwaffe: "How bloody dare they. They will pay for this!"

A family friend, Rosemary Pepler, later recalled of the machine-gunning incident that it occurred one Sunday lunchtime and that three [sic] German aeroplanes passed over Ditchling High Street, "...almost skimming the roof tops", and then fired towards Mabel and the children as she sat in a deckchair in the garden of relatives at Laine End. Given these facts, it is reasonable to assume that the aircraft were the Dornier 17s of 9./KG76 which had passed at extremely low level over the area at lunchtime on Sunday 18 August, heading to attack RAF Kenley, as it was then recorded that the raiders machine-gunned various locations as they passed overhead.

It was an episode which had very much frightened Mabel, and Richard inevitably began to question why on earth he had got the family out of Croydon to the countryside – an erstwhile peaceful countryside which was now at the epicentre of the Battle of Britain. Damn! Why did he get them out of Croydon? Would that have not been safer? After all, it was rumoured that Hitler had ordered Croydon to be left untouched. Untouched so that he could arrive there in triumph when Britain was conquered. And yet, Richard's answer came later when he heard that on 15 August, Croydon had already been bombed and heavy casualties sustained. The truth of the matter, then, was that nowhere was safe. And the truth of the matter was also that Richard Stevens could do nothing to defend his family flying a Percival Q6, Short Scion or Puss Moth in quiet little circuits around the Midlands.

If anything, the machine-gunning episode was the catalyst to propel Richard to yet further efforts to secure his posting to fighters. Playing into his hands and helping to negate somewhat the issues relating to his age was the considerable attrition rate of killed or wounded then being suffered by RAF Fighter Command as it fought the Battle of Britain. Already, pilots had been drafted in from other commands on volunteering – including Bomber, Coastal, Training and Transport – as well as naval fighter pilots being attached from the Fleet Air Arm to bolster against these losses. Undoubtedly, it was this desperate situation which saw Richard's name finally being added to the list of pilots selected for training at an operational training unit, preparatory to joining Fighter Command. When his brother, James, briefly asked of Richard some while after

Dornier 17-Z bombers of 9./KG 76 approach Beachy Head at low level on Sunday, 18 August 1940. Minutes later, they were strafing the area around Ditchling where Mabel and the twins were sitting in a garden. The episode enraged Richard and became one of the motivating factors in his drive to 'get back' at the Germans.

he had become a fighter pilot why it was that he hadn't been 'streamed' towards being a bomber pilot, especially in view of his experience of multi-engine flying at night, and given his age, Richard just replied gruffly: "Wrong temperament!"

But if Richard's dream to become a fighter pilot was about to be realised, his personal life was also about to be shattered.

Once more, the telephone rang in the orderly room and again a runner was sent to urgently find Sergeant Stevens. It was 1 October 1940. Rushing to the telephone and taking the call, Richard could hardly piece together what was being said to him, or even who was saying it. All he could comprehend was "...an accident" and "...Frances was badly burned" and then "...died of shock". In an instant, his life all but fell apart. Nothing could be done to console him in his grief as he locked himself in his room for hours on end, and wept.

The funeral, when it was held about a week later, was in the municipal cemetery at Hove in East Sussex. After Frances' little white coffin was lowered into the grave, Richard turned on his heels and, alone, he walked briskly away from the small party of mourners. Head down, he marched out of the cemetery gates and vanished from sight. It was the last time that Mabel would ever see him.

It was this tragic episode that directly gave rise to the story about Mabel, Frances and John all being killed during the Blitz and one which Richard himself perpetuated on many occasions. There were also variations to that story, including that just the children had been killed, and that Mabel had 'lost her mind'. Those variations also placed the tragedy in different locations; London, Manchester or Bath. It all depended which newspaper, author or publisher would later print stories about Richard. The reality, though, was that Frances had died in a tragic domestic accident which seems not to be have been even remotely linked to enemy action.

Richard's brother, James, would later recall: "As to it being caused by enemy action, we didn't have any such ideas at the time. It was considered to have been an accident. As simple as that."

His Majesty's district coroner, F W Butler Esq., also concurred. The brief and succinct official reports set out the detail:

"PC Elliott reports the death of Frances Marie Stevens, aged 21 months, of No.2 Oaklands Farm Cottages, Shermanbury, which occurred at 9 a.m. on Tuesday 1 October 1940 at the above address, the

The grave of little Frances at Hove, East Sussex, which also commemorates her doting father, Richard Stevens. Note the mis-spelling of 'Playne'.

apparent cause of which was shock due to burns caused by burning paraffin through the upsetting of a stove used for heating purposes. The facts were reported to the coroner, F W Butler Esq, who decided to hold an inquest at 3 p.m. on Thursday 3 October 1940, at 'Sevenoaks', Shermanbury, sitting without a jury."

Then:

"The coroner, sitting without a jury, held an inquest at the time, date and place stated above and after hearing the evidence of witnesses, and that of Dr Dickens, reached a verdict of: 'Death due to shock following severe burning caused by the overturning of a paraffin oil heater. Accident.'"

In accord with James Stevens' recall, there was not any suggestion of enemy action having caused the accident, either directly or indirectly. On that date, in that location and at the material time, no air raid warning was in operation and there was no enemy air activity over the region until around 2.30 p.m. when a Messerschmitt 109 was shot down at Falmer, not too far away, and just to the north of Brighton. Any suggestion that this episode could in some way be related can be dismissed as some five-and-a-half hours separates the two incidents. The tragic event, then, cannot be attributed to enemy action, notwithstanding the popular version of events which would emerge later.

Quite simply, Mabel had left the house briefly to hang out some washing to dry, leaving the twins playing happily indoors. Whatever took place, it happened quickly. When she returned to the cottage moments later it was to the sound of screams and cries from the twins and Mabel found the paraffin stove had somehow been knocked over, the spilt fuel now flaming in blue tongues of fire around Frances and John. Extinguishing the flames, Mabel's training as a nurse kicked in. Unfortunately, and despite her medical knowledge, she was unable to do anything to save her daughter who died shortly afterwards from shock, while John – less badly burned – was taken to hospital where he soon recovered from his injuries.

It had been an awful accident, and not only did Mabel blame herself but her estranged husband, Richard, believed her to be in some way culpable. For a marriage already in crisis, this was the final straw. Now, Richard sensed that his only way forward, and to be able to hang on to his sanity, was to knuckle down and focus on his forthcoming fighter pilot training. His anger and despair would be channelled in that direction and that direction alone. And he would 'blame' the Germans. After all, it wouldn't have happened if this wretched war hadn't seen the family relocated to Shermanbury. If anything, though, it had been the earlier machine-gunning episode which had so riled Richard against the foe.

On 29 October 1940, less than three weeks after the funeral for little Frances, Sergeant Richard Playne Stevens, 740527, reported for duty with 56 Operational Training Unit at RAF Sutton Bridge in Lincolnshire. Nobody could even begin to imagine what this stocky, slightly overweight and relatively 'old' pilot would go on to achieve inside the next 12 months.

Originally, 56 OTU had been numbered 6 OTU, which itself had been formed out of what was previously known as 11 Group Pilot Pool. The purpose of the pool was twofold: first, to bring pilots posted from flying training schools up to the standard of fully trained fighter pilots prior to posting to operational squadrons, and, second, to train RAFVR pilots who had completed 120 hours solo and were willing to devote time to learn the operational side of fighter piloting (NB: the latter only applied pre-war).

Frances Stevens in a colourised portrait kept by Richard as a precious keepsake after her death.

RAF Sutton Bridge during the summer of 1940 with Hurricanes of the operational training unit ranged on the grass in the foreground. It was here that Richard embarked on the path towards becoming a fighter pilot.

Here, at 56 OTU, students on the course were put through what were roughly six-week courses where they became familiar with the Hurricane and flying fighter tactics, the instructors being experienced fighter pilots who were being rested from operations. During the spring of 1940, for instance, many of those instructors were successful fighter pilots who had served during the Battle of France and were now passing on their knowledge and experience to the new boys coming through the system. In the case of Richard Stevens, his instructors were pilots who had until just recently served on front-line fighter squadrons during the Battle of Britain. One of Richard's instructors was Flight Lieutenant Derek Dowding (son of Air Chief Marshal Sir Hugh Dowding) who had flown an operational tour with 74 Squadron during the Dunkirk period and early part of the Battle of Britain. Among others, Derek Dowding was now training men like Richard to become fighter pilots in light of his father's diktat to release pilots from other commands to bolster Fighter Command.

His recall of Richard Stevens was clear:

> "R P Stevens comes back to me as someone outstanding in the flow of trainees who came through my hands at that time. We were the last link in the training chain, dealing 100 per cent with young, very inexperienced pilots. I myself was only 21, trying to teach 19 or 20-year-olds the wisdom gained from just one tour of operations.

"Onto this scene burst the 32-year-old Stevens, vastly more experienced than any of his instructors. The difference was, I suppose, that we could fly Hurricanes and he could not.

"As has been expressed by others, he was not a particularly delicate pilot. But he had this very unusual ability to 'use' the aircraft for his own particular ends. He was an incredibly competent bad weather pilot, but curiously inept at the very last stage of the landing. Whether this was some curious anomaly in his sight, which could not cope with the normal landing process, but which gave him exceptional night vision I do not know.

"As an individual, he was curiously ungracious in a manner which did not add to his popularity in the mess. Of course, there was the age and experience difference. I just think that his time at Sutton Bridge was a not very welcome interruption in his programme of getting to work on his vendetta with the Germans. We could, of course, teach him to fly the Hurricane inside a week but the 'system' demanded that he should stay the full course. Most of this was completely unnecessary in his case and may have contributed to his impatience.

A Hurricane of 56 OTU at Sutton Bridge in 1940. This aircraft, L2006, is marked in standard camouflage colours, but with a red fuselage band and yellow undersides. Richard first flew a Hurricane at Sutton Bridge in early November 1940. By the end of that month he had joined an operational fighter squadron and was well on the road to becoming a fighter 'ace' two months later.

"I cannot say that I liked him. But I was much impressed by his ability and his dedication. I think we needed 'killers' at that time. And he most certainly was one."

Squadron Leader Harold Maguire was then CO in charge of flying at 56 OTU having commanded 229 Squadron during the Battle of Britain. In common with others, he recalled Richard's brusque nature and a personality that was "sparing of words". Maguire went on to add that:

"His obsessive hatred of the German air force was quite true, and his fanaticism very obvious. In fact, he applied for nightfighters on leaving – most unusual for a Hurricane pilot. Also, it is important to realise there was no specialist nightfighter training units and he would have done minimal night flying with us. He just wanted to go to nightfighters. But he did tell me that his family had been killed in a night-time air raid on South London. Before the war I think he had accumulated something like 3,000 flying hours."

For Richard, the course had concluded by 26 November – a little under a month since being posted to Sutton Bridge, although he had already been commissioned as pilot officer on 4 November. On leaving the operational training unit, the instructors and fellow course members didn't expect much would come of this rather 'elderly' would-be fighter pilot. Secretly, many thought he wouldn't last five minutes. And none of them ever expected to hear of him again.

Chapter Four

FIGHTER PILOT

It was a little under two months since the tragic death of Frances that Richard had 'passed out' from 56 OTU at Sutton Bridge for his first and much longed-for operational posting, albeit a posting over which the shadow of Frances' loss fell overwhelmingly on her father. Such was his palpable grief, and such was the unusual persona of this older-than-average pilot (he was 32) who strode into the officers' mess at RAF Wittering in November 1940 to join 151 Squadron, that fellow pilots quickly knew to avoid him. Here was not the typically rumbustious young pilot out of the usual mould. Not a youngster eager to play hard and drink hard in his precious off-duty hours, or to go galivanting around after pretty girls in a flashy sports car. Not for him was the carefree 'live for today because tomorrow I might be dead' attitude which was prevalent among many of his younger fellow pilots. Instead, here was a somewhat withdrawn, intense, serious and noticeably solitary man with precious few social skills or graces – and a man who was deadly earnest and focussed about the task in hand. Those who cautiously tried to get close, or attempted to get to know him better, usually got very short shrift. One such was Flight Lieutenant Irving 'Black' Smith, who recalled:

Flight Lieutenant Irving 'Black' Smith, 151 Squadron.

"Stevens was certainly different to all the rest. I couldn't say that I particularly liked him. But I really admired him. And I particularly admired his determination and his drive to get at the 'Hun', especially when I learned his tragic story about his wife and two children being killed during the Blitz. I think the story was told once – to me – and then all the rest of us knew and understood. And we left him alone, to his solitary quietness, because of it."

Later, much later, the author H E Bates would write extensively of Stevens. Of him, he said: "It is often the quietest who hate the most, and his

The pilots and air gunners of 151 Squadron line up for a group photo at RAF Wittering in front of one of the squadron's Defiant aircraft. Richard is seated fifth from left and Squadron Leader Adams (the squadron's CO) is seated centre with the dog at his left.

reticence was very typical. It really concealed a great ferocity."

As we now know, Richard's 'tragic story' did not happen the way he described it. But it was a story which he seemingly encouraged, allowing it to propagate within the squadron, within the service and, later, with the press. Leastways, he did little or nothing to rectify the story now being put about, and which even those who served with him and who survived the war continued to believe. Quite likely, the rather private man who was Richard used the story as a cover to explain his almost anti-social behaviour and to encourage others to go away and not to bother him or to pry; and surely to fuel his hatred of the enemy. That was all very well, but once Richard became celebrated and feted by the news media, he could hardly refute the story he had himself initiated. Consequently, it became one which was so often repeated that it has almost become an established historical 'fact', albeit with variations of detail.

Another of those who repeated what was a differently embellished version of the tale was nightfighter pilot Roderick Chisholm, CBE, DSO, DFC in his book *Cover of Darkness* (Chatto & Windus, 1953):

> "Stevens, who had the top score...landed at Coltishall early one morning [almost certainly during late June, 1941]. His had been a remarkable achievement, for he had destroyed 13 enemy aircraft with no more assistance than his own intelligence and eyesight could give. Operating freelance in a long-

range Hurricane [sic], he flew as one possessed; he had a simple mission and no conflicting interests. It was said that his children had been killed in the Blitz and that his wife had lost her reason. He scorned Beaufighters and radar, but we had interesting talks with him."

Richard had spun his story and let it go, unchecked and uncorrected. However, it is clear that he had now separated from (or was estranged from) Mabel, having little if nothing more to do with her or the surviving twin before his eventual death. Those within his family felt that, in some way, he had likely blamed Mabel for the tragic accident which had taken the life of little Frances. Also, they felt that he simply couldn't emotionally deal with the loss of his precious Frances and that distancing himself from his wife and the surviving child was perhaps all part of his coping strategy. That, and throwing himself into his career as a fighter pilot. Certainly, it was the case that the 'tragic story' meant his fellow pilots wouldn't ever pry or raise such a sensitive matter with him again. And that suited him perfectly. At least the painful subject of his daughter, and the estrangement from his wife, would not have to be confronted. To an extent, of course, there was an element of truth to the story in that Frances had died, although the elaboration to include his wife and both children was an extremely exaggerated version of events. The story, however, was all very well as one kept within the confines of the squadron and the service. But it was not long before it had a much wider and a very public audience. What Mabel thought of the matter, however, is not recorded. That said, and returning to H E Bates, that author did at least get the facts correct in that it was just his daughter who died when he later wrote:

> "When the Nazis became responsible for the death of his daughter during the Blitz there was no longer anything to be done with him. He became one of those legendary figures that read alone in their rooms and fret to be flying and curse the controller and the weather: one of those who ask only to be free for revenge, who are slightly insane in their desire to equal the score and who are talked about in messes long after they are dead.
>
> "They are the sort of individualists – sometimes exiles, sometimes men with lost limbs – whom you seem to find always among the nightfighters. They are those who, because they have lost countries or limbs or families or perhaps hope, do not want very much to be disciplined. The war for them has become very personal. For them, night is more free than day: free darkness, free stars, free moon, free space for the expression for a feud. They find raiders in the moon above low cloud, shadows in the solar flare of ack-ack and above the glare of ground fires."

In almost every respect, Bates exactly encapsulated Richard the man and he was right to say that Frances had died 'during' the Blitz. But not because of it or because of enemy action.

Having regard to Richard's exceptional night vision and his truly remarkable night-flying capabilities, somebody in the Air Ministry postings section had clearly made a shrewd decision in posting him to 151 Squadron, a dedicated nightfighter unit which, unusually, flew a mix of Hurricanes and Defiants. Doubtless, this would have been influenced by end of course appraisal reports from 56 OTU where his instructors were keen that his abilities were exploited to the full. However, it is important to understand that Richard was never 'trained' as a nightfighter pilot. Such training didn't exist and the system, the OTUs, simply turned out fighter pilots who were posted to operational fighter squadrons with a satisfactory degree of flying and fighting competence. Nightfighting was learnt on the job, as it were. In this, of course, Stevens already had the edge over others who might have been similarly posted, given his extensive night and bad weather flying experience.

Marshal of the Royal Air Force William Sholto Douglas.

Almost implying that fighter pilots should have no real difficulty in finding nocturnal targets, experiments in December 1940 had already shown that pilots in aircraft operating at night, high above target areas, could quite easily pick out enemy aircraft below. In his Despatch, Marshal of the Royal Air Force Sir Sholto Douglas, wrote:

> "On the night of 11th December, I tried out for the second time, a measure which had previously been given an inconclusive trial over Bristol. Twenty Hampden bombers were sent to patrol at various specified heights over Birmingham during a concentrated attack on that city. The crews reported seeing a large number of enemy aircraft, but the Hampdens were too unwieldy to bring any of them to action. This experience proved, however, that in suitable circumstances interception by purely visual means was possible."

All of this, however, rather overlooked the complex difficulties involved in fighting at night in a single-seat fighter as we shall see later in this work. However, Flight Lieutenant 'Black' Smith summed up Richard's posting and the 'art' of the nightfighter:

> "We were in the kingdom of the blind at this stage, with the majority of pilots being more concerned about not flying into the ground rather than looking for enemy aircraft. Then, onto this scene walked one Pilot Officer R P Stevens, older than any of us and vastly more experienced as a pilot. We had freedom

On 29 November 1940, Richard flew this cannon-armed Hurricane, L1750, which was the first Hurricane he flew on 151 Squadron. L1750 was something of a 'hybrid' aircraft with its underslung 20-mm cannon pods. It was one of the earliest cannon-equipped Hurricanes to serve with RAF Fighter Command.

of flight, but none of us put it to so much good as he did."

Four days after his official posting to 151 Squadron, Richard began flying the squadron Hurricanes, his first flight being recorded on 29 November 1940 when he flew Hurricane L1750 in a 30-minute flight from Wittering to Digby, before taking V6634 from Digby to Bramcote immediately after. Sadly, none of his logbooks – either service or civilian – have survived but it is possible to construct his operational RAF flying record from squadron operations record books. (Interesting to note, too, that Hurricane L1750, DZ – Z, was the first experimentally cannon-armed Hurricane which had been operated by 151 Squadron throughout the Battle of Britain.)

After his flight on 29 November, there followed a protracted series of local familiarisation flights. All of them, bar two on 9 and 17 December, were flown during daylight hours and included sector recce flights, formation flying, practice attacks and the like. All of it was standard fare, of course, for the average pilot newly joining an operational squadron direct from OTU. Except that Richard wasn't your average pilot, of course – just as 'Black' Smith had intimated; and he, after all, was anxious to get cracking. Finally, on 21 December, came his chance with a night patrol between 22.20 and 00.15. Frustratingly, nothing was seen. It was the same again when he flew a patrol between 04.20 and 06.35 on 23 December.

Of flying the Hurricane at night, operationally, on 151 Squadron Flight Lieutenant Smith provides us with some perspective of what it was like for men such as Smith and Stevens:

"In October 1940, 151 Squadron had, along with several other Hurricane squadrons, been re-designated as a nightfighter squadron and re-equipped with Defiants. We objected strongly to this move, but we were told to shut up and get on with it. But as a sop to our views that the Defiant was useless because of its poor performance, light armament and severe tactical limita-

A 151 Squadron group photo, this time including pilots, gunners and ground crew with a squadron Hurricane. Richard, however, does not appear to feature in this picture.

Defiant pilots and air gunners of 151 Squadron pictured during the winter of 1940/41. Their combined successes did not equal the total score of just one of the squadron's Hurricane pilots, Richard Stevens.

tions, we were finally allowed to keep about 12 of our Mk 1 Hurricanes. We were a highly unusual RAF fighter squadron in that respect as we operated a mix of aircraft – Defiants and Hurricanes.

"As an aircraft, the Hurricane was balanced on a pin and could not be left alone to fly itself. These characteristics made for great manoeuvrability, of value by day, but this was an extremely distracting factor at night – particularly for inexperienced pilots. We also flew with our canopies open for better visibility, but that let in the roar of the exhaust as well as carbon monoxide. There was no heating in the aircraft and at 20,000 feet in winter the temperature could be -55 Centigrade, so cold that it seriously degraded one's ability to function. One pilot was so cold that when he caught a Heinkel over Birmingham he couldn't even manage to press the firing button. I can remember the tears of frustration running down his face after he had landed.

"When one reads the combat reports of us nightfighter boys at that time, it is quite important to bear in mind that we weren't just battling the Germans!"

December was a period when Richard actually piloted (three times) one of the squadron's Defiant aircraft which was noted as 'Experience on Type', as well as two relatively short hops between Bramcote and Wittering. Although flights by him on the squadron's Defiants continued sporadically into the new year, none are recorded as operational. One, though, was a flight as 'passenger' (i.e. in the gun turret) with Flight Lieutenant Desmond McMullen the pilot of N3371 when the pair flew to Ringway, Wolverhampton and return on 9 January 1941, with Richard having positioned himself in the gun turret. The Defiant flights with Richard as pilot were recorded, variously, as local flying, formation flying and one as an interception exercise. If anything, it seems that the Defiant was not only unpopular with the other squadron pilots, but it suited neither Richard nor his temperament. And exactly what he thought of his stocky frame being squeezed into the gun turret of one is not recorded! Not for him was the manoeuvring of an aircraft into a position for his gunner to engage the enemy, and his flight as turret passenger must have convinced him of this. Quite apart from not lik-

A Defiant of 151 Squadron with distinctive shark's-mouth insignia. Although Richard Stevens flew the aircraft several times, he never did so on operational flights. He disliked the Defiant intensely, and was vocal in his opinion of it. Unusually, 151 Squadron had a mix of both Hurricanes and Defiant aircraft in 1941.

ing the Defiant, neither did he much like the idea of flying in combat with a third party.

As to the mix of Defiant and Hurricane aircraft on 151 Squadron, the operations record book later noted on 30 January 1941: "Today, the squadron split into three flights, two of Defiants and one of Hurricanes, the object being to prove the Hurricane a better nightfighter than the Defiant."

As 1940 drew to a close, however, Richard must have been frustrated that he had yet to get to grips with the enemy; it was a frustration doubtless heightened as Hitler boasted of the night raids on Britain: "They will be waged with all the determination and courage which is at our disposal."

All Richard wanted to do was to play his part in countering them. For the sake of Frances, if nothing else. And to counter the raids with all of *his* own courage and determination. On Christmas Eve, though, he flew what was seemingly a futile daytime flight, logged as 'Dogfighting Training'. Futile because the sort of operations on which he was about to embark were not about daylight flying at all, or of dogfighting. It was all about night flying, and of hunting by stealth and guile. Dogfighting didn't come into it. It must surely have further heightened his frustration, deepening a blackening mood as he went into his first Christmas without Frances or the comfort of family around him.

For Fighter Command as a whole, though, the situation in respect of countering the Luftwaffe's night blitz was as desperate as it was depressing. Thus far, no really effective nightfighting force had been established. Airborne interception (AI) radar was in its infancy, and it was only in the previous November that Flight Lieutenant John Cunningham of 604 Squadron had achieved the first AI-assisted 'kill' over land. Under the circumstances, then, it was very small comfort for the British people to learn, as *Aeroplane* magazine noted, that: "…so ends a year with night bombing on both sides, and neither side has any defence against it." Against this gloomy background, Richard was stepping into the arena of nightfighting. Prime Minister Winston Churchill reacted to the enemy's threats with typically powerful and pithy words: "You do your worst, and we will do our best."

At Wittering, Pilot Officer Richard Stevens was about to step up to meet Churchill's promise. However, as December moved into January, and across what was a particularly severe winter period, the month dawned with yet more local flying, formation flying and further occasional daytime flying in Defiants. Finally, and after what were logged as 'Night Flying Tests' on two consecutive nights, 14 and 15 January, Richard's war began on the night of 16 January. It was time, at last, for him to "do his best".

On the first of two patrols, Richard took off in Hurricane V6934 from RAF Wittering at 01.00 hours. Overall, and despite the severe winter, the night was brightly lit by moonlight but with variable cloud and snow showers, although visibility was recorded as 'good'. What happened next is concisely set out in what was Pilot Officer Richard Stevens' first combat report:

When Flight Lieutenant John Cunningham brought down the first enemy aircraft over land by using airborne interception radar on 20 November 1940, his success was attributed to his 'Cat's Eyes' vision in order to conceal the existence of the airborne radar equipment. The wreckage of Cunningham's victim, a Junkers 88, is seen here at West Wittering, Sussex. Cunningham would later admit that the only true 'Cat's Eyes' nightfighter was Richard Stevens.

A Flight 151 Squadron
Do 215 [sic]
Attacked at 01.35 over East London, enemy aircraft at 20,000 ft, climbing to 30,000 ft.

On instructions from control at Wittering I was vectored south and enemy aircraft reported as approaching from starboard. I observed bomb bursts and AA fire to the south. Continuing my vector I saw shell smoke at 19,000 ft then observed enemy aircraft above and gave chase eastwards. Enemy aircraft climbed away to 30,000 ft, leaving contrails from 25,000ft upwards. I closed in behind and pulled the plug. I closed in behind and below making use of cover from the condensation trails at 25 yards. I swung out and delivered a quarter attack. No return fire experienced and shots seen striking engine, centre section and fuselage. Enemy aircraft dived steeply down to 3,000 ft. I followed. Enemy aircraft pulled up and I gave one short burst at approx. 250 yards beam attack – at same time enemy aircraft burst properly into flames and crashed into a wood just outside

Wreckage of the Dornier 17-Z at Hartswood, Brentwood, on the morning of 16 January 1941. This was the first of Richard's long tally of 'kills'.

Hornchurch village. I did not see any chutes, and circling crash at 100 ft I observed no survivors. Enemy aircraft completely burnt out.

I used reflector gun sight fully dimmed for beginning of burst, but as vibration turned this out, I continued with the bead foresight.

His victim had, in fact, been a Dornier 17-Z of 4./KG3, 5K + DM, W.Nr. 3456, with its NCO crew of Uffz M Schindler, Uffz J Sanktjohanser, Uffz L Winkler and Gefr W Teichmann, all of whom were killed when their aircraft plunged into woodland at Hartswood, Brentwood, and smashed itself to pieces among the trees, driving much of the wreckage deep underground. However, Richard's spree of success was not yet over for the night, although it was the Brentwood 'kill' which had been witnessed by many on the ground below. One of them was Albert Shoebridge of Woodman Road, Brentwood (see page 13).

Reading of Richard's exploits that night, Shoebridge was delighted to discover that he hailed from his hometown, Tunbridge Wells, and wrote a congratulatory letter to his parents on 24 February 1941:

"May I be permitted to congratulate you on your son's recent exploit, the exploit for which he has been decorated; shooting two Huns down in one night.

The reason I am writing is because of some sort of coincidence – his first victim crashed about 400 yards from my house, in a wood at the end of the road. His name everybody here has quoted as though he was known personally to them, but on having an *Advertiser* sent to me I find that he hails from my native town. Well, I feel more than bucked.

According to eyewitnesses personally known to me, he did his job well. On his tail, then a bank, and up from beneath and that finished it.

The Hun started to dive from the moon (from here), circled round twice then crashed. He left his smoke trail behind him.

I didn't notice his first spiral but his second woke me up out of my lethargic attitude to the alert which had only just been sounded about 1.30 am. He crashed immediately afterwards, and I was out in time to see the fighter banking round to make sure he was down.

We see quite a lot of the RAF fighters here. They are all fine lads and we often wish them luck as they go over.

So, 'Bless 'em all'.

And may your son have many more 'brace of birds' to his credit.

Yours sincerely,

A H Shoebridge."

Mr Shoebridge's account matches almost exactly Richard's combat report, in particular seeing the Hurricane come down low to observe the wreckage on the ground. What the writer did not know, however, was that in the dive, Hurricane V6934 had potentially been over-stressed and was immediately grounded when he landed back at Wittering at 02.10 hours. Not mentioned in his combat report, however, is the fact that Richard had temporarily 'blacked out' from excessive 'G' in the dive from 30,000 ft. Worse, he had painfully injured an eardrum in that all-out dive but nevertheless remained at readiness for the remainder of the night. Then, and notwithstanding his ear problem, he was sent off on yet another patrol at 04.25 hours. This time, though, it was in Hurricane V7496, with V6934 temporarily grounded. Again, we turn to Richard's combat report for the detail of what transpired:

```
A Flight 151 Squadron
He 111
Attacked at 04.53 over East London. Enemy aircraft at 19,000 ft.
```

```
Acting on vectors from Control at Wittering I flew south and
informed of bandit approaching from starboard at 18,000 ft. Pro-
ceeding in a series of S turns I observed bandit behind - posi-
tion north of London. Continuing turn, bandit banked away from
me. Searchlights then picked up both of us and I took up position
behind and below bandit. Closed, and at 50-25 yards delivered
quarter attack. Return fire observed from top of enemy aircraft.
Breaking away to short distance I repeated former attack, deliv-
ering ten bursts in all from both sides. Enemy aircraft observed
```

smoking and saw white smoke from starboard motor and losing
height. Two of bandit's crew baled out after first two attacks. I
followed bandit down to 2,000 ft and lost sight of him when making
turn to reduce forward speed. Position near Southend. I consider
Wittering Control very instrumental in success of this intercept.

Bead foresight used.

Not hit by enemy aircraft.

Two guns did not fire.

In this instance, Richard's quarry was a Heinkel He 111-H of 2./KG53, A1 + JK, W.Nr 3638, which eventually went into the sea near Spit Buoy off Holehaven, Canvey Island. As it crashed, taking with it Uffz H Graf, it struck a barge and partially submerged. However, the wreck was eventually recovered for examination. Of the remainder of the crew, Ltn G Möhring, Gefr T Lübking and Gefr E Henduck all baled out to be taken POW, although Richard had only seen two of the crew escape on their parachutes.

In the Air Intelligence A.I.1(g) technical assessment of the wreck it was stated: "The wreckage showed several strikes in the starboard wing and fuselage and in the airscrews of both engines."

By now, it had gone 5 a.m. and the weather had begun to turn decidedly inclement (the operations record book for 151 Squadron simply noted: "Weather duff.") such that Richard diverted to nearby RAF Gravesend instead of heading back to Wittering. At 05.30 hours, having been instructed to head for the nearest nightfighter airfield, which was Gravesend, he circled the field and was given a green Aldis lamp flashing the Morse code letters of the day in reply to his white identity flashes of that night, before the Glim lamp[2] flarepath was switched on and he was then guided in by the floodlit Chance Light. Taxiing in, he made his way to the red, green and white taxi post, from where he was marshalled in by two white torches being revolved by the duty airman, directing him to the refuel and re-arm points.

Finally, he was down. With the Hurricane switched off, Richard stumped into the dispersal building to find exhausted Defiant pilots and gunners of 141 Squadron lounging around and doing nothing. One of the pilots was Pilot Officer Ivor Cosby who recalled:

---

2   A Glim lamp flarepath was a single line of ten electric lamps, set at 100-yard intervals, with two other lamps across the end of the row set out as a 'T' shape. Aircraft took off or landed with the 'Glims' to the port side. The lamps were connected by a single cable which was powered from a starter accumulator trolley (a 'Trolleyacc' in RAF parlance of the day) which could quickly be powered on or off on instruction from flying control. At airfields like Gravesend, for example, there were no R/T facilities, and after being ordered off by telephone, pilots had to often climb to something like 3,000 feet before they could communicate with sector ops over frequently ineffectual HF radios. As Ivor Cosby later commented: "It was all very primitive. And bloody dangerous!"

Top: Richard's second victim on the night of 15/16 January 1941 was this Heinkel 111, downed in the sea off Canvey Island, Essex. Bottom: Richard Stevens landed at RAF Gravesend after his second victory on the night of 15/16 January, having been prevented to return to RAF Wittering by inclement weather. This photo was taken in 1940 and shows pilots of 66 Squadron relaxing in the dispersal room between sorties.

"Suddenly, in strode a chap wearing an Irvin jacket and flying boots. Looking around at us he demanded: 'Why aren't you lot airborne?' He was told in no uncertain words of one syllable and quite a few expletives what he could do! We asked him who the hell he was, where he came from, and in what. He told us from Wittering, and in a Hurricane. So we told him to bloody well go back there. He said his name was Stevens. We had never heard of him."

Richard had already bought into the adage from Sector, Group and Command HQ that: "If the Hun is flying, so can you!"

It wouldn't be long before the pilots of 141 Squadron and everyone else would hear of him, and it was possibly a teleprinter signal from HQ Fighter Command to HQ 12 Group on 17 January that set in motion a chain of events which would not only see Richard lauded in the press but also awarded a DFC for his actions that night. The signal read:

"Following from Chief of Air Staff to C-in-C HQ Fighter Command. Please convey my congratulations to P/O Stevens of 151 Squadron on the resolution and efficiency displayed by him in his two successful combats last night. No. 151 Squadron may well pride themselves that they so worthily maintain a reputation for nightfighting."

As the teleprinters were clattering their message, however, Richard was only now – at 14.40 hours the next day – clambering into his Hurricane at Gravesend to fly back to

The teleprinted congratulatory message from the Chief of the Air Staff on 17 January 1941, recognising the achievement of Richard Stevens' double victory.

Wittering. After landing at Gravesend following his second victory, the weather had well and truly socked in. Doubtless the aircrew of 141 Squadron, against whom Richard had rather unfairly railed, were secretly pleased that the weather had closed in so badly that even the gung-ho intrepid Hurricane jockey from 12 Group couldn't get off the ground. In all truth and taking into consideration his ability in even the foulest of conditions, the weather must have been pretty awful to have kept him at Gravesend for so many hours. In fact, it was more than awful back at Wittering, too, and had he tried to get back there then it is possible that even he, the maestro in darkness and foul weather, would have found it challenging. It had already caused his CO, Squadron Leader J S Adams, to come unstuck.

After Richard returned that night following his first 'kill', he went straight to the ops room. There, he found his CO and the pair discussed enemy aircraft plots which were still active on the general situation map to the west of their sector. After discussion with the sector controller, it was agreed that the pair should take off for a further sortie. However, writing in the 1980s, Adams confessed:

> "Delighted as I was with the addition of another victory to the squadron's credit, inwardly I had to admit that my delight was tinged with jealousy and frustration. When I congratulated him, he made it sound easy; no fuss or confusion; just a sighting, an accurate aim, a burst of cannon fire [sic] and it was all over."

Doubtless, it all conspired to make Adams enthuse about going off bomber-hunting. After all, there were plots on the table and, at that moment, the night-flying conditions were good. And he couldn't let one of his junior officers take all the glory. Pride, as they say, cometh before a fall – and the night would not end well for Adams. Perhaps, though, he was just not suited to the nightfighter role, let alone leading a nightfighter squadron, as his candid admissions later revealed:

> "I found take-off and the climb into darkness something of an ordeal since the outbreak of war. I could fly reasonably well on my instruments, but I was painfully aware that my eyesight deteriorated rapidly by night. I did what I could to improve matters, but large quantities of vitamin A tablets, the wearing of dark glasses before take-off and other measures seemed to have no effect. When I taxied out...the familiar feeling of tension mounted; the void in the pit of the stomach, the effort required to steady the voice and the unnatural chill that seemed to engulf me."

The CO's situation and ability were as far removed from Richard's as they possibly could be. And that in no way reflects on Adams' suitability or acumen as a fighter pilot (he had served in the Battle of Britain and had already earned a DFC), or as a squadron commander. Just that, like so many others who were posted to nightfighter squadrons, he was not a natural nightfighter pilot. Square pegs and round holes. Already, he had come perilously close to shooting down a Wellington accidentally just a few nights earlier. On this night, though, he found no enemy bombers with which to match Richard's earlier victory. Instead, he found just an empty sky, then, as he returned to Wittering he encountered rolling cloud and dreadfully poor visibility – such that he had no idea where he was, couldn't find the airfield and eventually baled out of

Roland Beamont in the cockpit of his Typhoon, pictured later in the war.

his Hurricane near Uppingham having run out of fuel. Taken back to the station sick-bay, it must have been humiliating, and yet a further frustration, to learn of Richard's second 'kill' that night.

Another dayfighter Hurricane pilot who had fought during the Battle of Britain and was allocated a nightfighting role across the 1940-1941 period was Flight Lieutenant Roland Beamont. On hearing that his 87 Squadron was to be assigned to full-time nightfighting duties, Beamont was not a little dismayed. Later, he would give a candid appraisal of the situation, what it meant to fight at night in Hurricanes and some of the difficulties involved. It also paints us considerably more of a picture of the world which Richard then inhabited and the challenges he needed to master.

As Beamont recalled:

> "This prospect seemed disastrous to a bunch of dayfighter pilots who had not only survived the two great air defence actions of the war so far but had done so with a very positive share in the ultimate victory. As they now saw it, they had to give up the inspiring climbs in formation, into the brilliant skies above any cloud, to fight and throw back an arrogant enemy whose black-swastika'd hordes had daily trespassed over our land and homes. Instead, they would have to live a life of crouching in the dark in ill-heated huts, awaiting the call from 'Ops' to 'Patrol Line A at 10,000 feet' – an order which would lead to a lone flight in the darkness in whatever the weather happened to be when the

order was issued. And those conditions, at night, could be atrocious – especially for the fighter pilot who had only ever been trained to fly by day.

"But all was not well. There were no effective homing aids and each sortie had to be conducted by dead reckoning (watch and compass) navigation to and from the patrol line. So, the patrols were flown by timed runs on reciprocal headings and, in the case of all but the most skilled in pilot navigation, after one-and-a-half hours on patrol on a pitch-black night and over mist or cloud there were precious few pilots who had any idea of their position.

"In theory, a 'fix' should have been possible by triangulation on radio voice transmissions, but in practice our TR9 radios were so completely unreliable and sensitive that the nightfighter pilot would have to resort to setting the 'safety course' for his home beacon at the end of each patrol and, beginning a descent on a timed run, then hope to break out below cloud in sight of the welcoming beacon flashing the signal of his home airfield – or any other beacon or clue which would lead him to somewhere to land before his fuel ran out!

"Once on patrol, of course, it was a case of eye-balling with no radar through a thick glass screen surrounded by a heavy metal structure and the reflector gunsight with its bright and distracting aiming-point graticule when switched on. To sight and to hold on to another aircraft was supremely difficult. The majority of our few interceptions that winter were in fact on searchlight-illuminated targets.

"Nevertheless, the job was tackled with intense effort and professionalism and training carried out on every suitable night for those pilots on standby. This included trying to assess each other's limits of night visibility. The No. 2 would drop slowly astern of the leader until the latter's silhouette had been lost at about 400 yards, and then the blue exhaust flames became almost invisible. Inevitably, contact was sometimes lost, and in all these sorties DR navigation over a totally blacked-out countryside was the sole means of recovery to a safe landing.

"The enthralling vistas of the dayfighter pilot in the wide-open skies had been replaced for us in the confines of the dimly red-lit cockpit with often nothing distinguishable in the total darkness outside. Our whole existence seemed limited to this cramped space and to the thunderous vibrations of the Merlin engine on whose continued roar our life indeed depended – for, in our experience, parachute escape from the Hurricane was by no means an assured way out.

"Clear moonlight, or even very clear starlit nights were a pleasure, as navigation could generally be visual. However, in all other circumstances of darkness in mist, rain, thick cloud icing or even snow, uncertainty was dominant.

Sometimes, after casting around in the goldfish bowl of darkness, the murk to one side or ahead would begin to glow intermittently with the signal of the flashing home beacon. Then, it was turn up the cockpit rheostat, check the beacon signal against the beacon card for the bearing to the airfield, set the new course and begin final descent. Then, below 500 ft, the line of shrouded lamps appeared. Undercarriage and flaps down; sometimes a hurried S turn to line up, throttle closed, stick back, sparks each side from the throttled engine, then the thump of a hard arrival. Less frequently, at night, a gentle three-pointer.

"Getting safely back on the ground at night felt like deliverance. Nothing like a daytime landing, which was horses for courses in the sturdy Hurricane. Night landings were anything but horses for courses – however good one's piloting skills!"

It was into this night-time world, then, that Pilot Officer Richard Stevens, novice fighter pilot, had been propelled. And already he had mastered it.

Finally, after his Gravesend odyssey, Richard touched down at Wittering at 15.20 hours. However, not only was Hurricane V6934 now 'sick' from the previous night's action, but so too was the pilot himself.

By now, the problems with his eardrum began to manifest themselves rather more seriously, although it was not until after a night-flying test in Hurricane V6543 at 16.25 hours on the afternoon of 16 January that Stevens presented himself to the MO. His left ear was giving him a great deal of trouble, and by this time, in any event, he must have been exhausted. He had been on duty since dusk the previous evening, flown two gruelling patrols which both involved combat and had then been kicking his heels at Gravesend until mid-afternoon waiting for the weather to improve before returning to Wittering. Back at his home base, he was again preparing for night operations. It was surely fortuitous that he found himself referred at once to the RAF Hospital, Halton. To Richard, of course, this was just an interruption in his desire to get on with the job in hand. This was especially the case when the announcement of the award of a DFC came through whilst he was recuperating from his ear injury, its promulgation in the *London Gazette* prompting the first pieces of newspaper coverage – stories which were to be the catalyst for Mr Shoebridge's letter to the Stevens family, of course.

The citation, published in the *London Gazette* on 4 February 1941, read as follows:

"This officer has performed outstanding work on nightfighting operations during recent weeks. One night in January 1941, he shot down two hostile aircraft in the London area. In both these engagements he chased the enemy over 100 miles before destroying each at extremely short range. In one instance he followed the enemy aircraft almost to ground level from 30,000

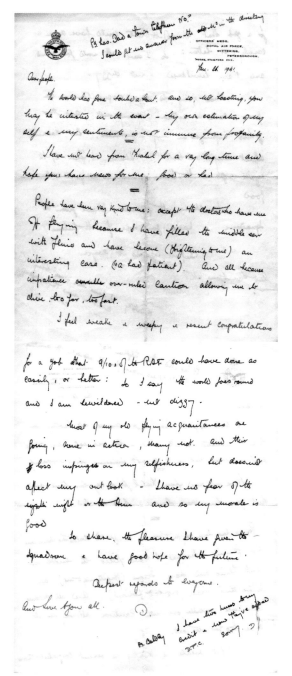

Richard's letter home to his family telling them of his success and award of the DFC.

feet. He has shown the utmost keenness and determination for operations in all conditions of weather."

However, whilst recuperating from his injury – and by now back at Wittering – he found time to write to his family on 26 January. Not least of all, it was to somewhat modestly alert the family to the award of a DFC, and although the *London Gazette* did not carry the citation until 4 February, announcements were made in the national press on 1 February. Thus, Richard's letter to his family was a timely one, albeit that its contents were both enigmatic and revealing. He wrote:

"Dear People,
The world has gone round-about. And so, not boasting, you may be interested in the event – my own estimation of myself and my sentiments are not immune from profanity.

I have not heard from Mabel for a very long time and hope you have news for me: good or bad.

People have been very kind to me: except the doctors who have kept me off flying because I have filled the middle ear with fluid and have become (frightening to me) an interesting case (i.e. a bad patient). And all because impatience over-ruled caution allowing me to dive too far, too fast.

I feel weak and weepy and resent congratulations for a job that 9/10 of the RAF could have done easily, or better: so, I say the world goes around and I am bewildered – but dizzy.

Most of my flying acquaintances are going, some in action, many not. And their loss impinges on my selfishness but doesn't affect my outlook. I have no fear of the night or the Hun and so my morale is good.

So, share the pleasure I have given the squadron and have good hope for the future. And love to all.

Dick.

PS: Baldly, I have two Huns to my credit and now they've added DFC. Sorry."

Not only is Richard's letter interesting for the factual detail it contains, but it also shows something of his mental state. Far from being the confident and steely-eyed hunter, driven to claw down enemy aircraft following the loss of Frances, we see a man who is emotional, self-critical and very unsure of himself. He even seems to feel unworthy of the DFC, going so far as to apologise to his family for the award of a medal and deeds he considers to be in no way exceptional. All that aside, however, he had very much been thrown into the public spotlight whether he liked it or not.

Almost immediately after the DFC announcement, the national newspapers began to pick up the story under headlines

Got Two Raiders In Night

THE R A F pilot who recently shot down two enemy night raiders in the London area in one night is Pilot Officer Richard Playne Stevens.

This was disclosed last night by the announcement that he has been awarded the D.F.C.

He chased each of the enemy machines for more than 100 miles in the darkness before destroying them at extremely short range.

In one instance he followed the raider almost to ground level from 30,000 feet (more than five miles up).

All Weathers

" He has shown the utmost keenness and determination for operations in all conditions of weather," says the official announcement.

Pilot-Officer Stevens was born at Tonbridge in 1909. Formerly a sergeant in the R A F, he was commissioned in the R A F V R last November. His wife lives at Ditchling, Sussex.

Almost at once, newspaper coverage of Richard's achievements began to appear. Throughout his short RAF career, he was the source of constant fascination for the news media – albeit that some of the reportage continued to peddle the line that he was driven to shoot down German aircraft because of the death of his wife and children in the Blitz.

such as 'Got Two Raiders in One Night', also referring to him as a 'Cat's Eyes' pilot. This was, of course, long after that sobriquet had been applied to Flight Lieutenant John Cunningham and used in that context publicly to cover the use of airborne interception radar (AI), implying that Cunningham had exceptional night vision. As we have already seen from John Cunningham's foreword to this book, he considered that it was Stevens who was the true 'Cat's Eyes' pilot. And with good cause, too.

Quite apart from the factual reportage, the *Daily Mail* ran a cartoon by Ronald Niebour ('Neb') early in 1941 which characterised Richard sitting cat-like, with cat's whiskers and eyes, in front of a bowl of milk while two other officers stand in the background, one explaining to the other: "He's one of the best nightfighter pilots we've got, old boy – can see like a cat in the dark." Later, Niebour sent the cartoon to Richard, inscribed: "With apologies to a real nightfighter DFC." Richard Stevens the nightfighter hero had arrived. His star was ascending in both the night skies over Britain and in the British press.

Interestingly, and in a wartime Air Ministry report on aspects of nightfighting, the view was:

"...and here perhaps it may as be well to try to assess the nightfighter's qualities. Much nonsense has been written of him and nothing has been more stupid, or has annoyed nightfighters more, than the journalistic catchword 'Cat's Eyes'. This suggests a pilot gifted with specialised qualities for seeing as well in the dark as he does by day and conjures the impression of a pilot glaring through the darkness like a fierce tomcat in search of hostile aircraft. Good night vision, though essential, is only one of many qualities demanded of the nightfighter."

—*Sketch by Neb.*

" He's one of the best night-fighter pilots we've got, old boy—can see like a cat in the dark."

Richard's exploits, and his 'Cat's Eyes' sobriquet, was the subject of this cartoon by Ronald Niebour ('Neb') in the Daily Mail.

In cases like Richard, however, such pilots – few although they were – were certainly operating on such a basis. Whatever the view of the author of that report, the 'Cat's Eyes' description of him was spot on. And, in his case, it *did* suggest quite accurately a pilot gifted with specialised qualities for seeing in the dark! Moreover, it wasn't 'one' of the qualities demanded of a nightfighter. It was *the* essential quality.

Of course, Richard was not yet an 'ace' – typi-

Looking every inch the archetypal fighter pilot, with his top button traditionally undone, Richard Stevens strikes a pose by his rather battered and oil-streaked Hurricane. Noteworthy are the anti-glare shields fitted between the exhaust stacks and the cockpit to protect the pilot from being dazzled by exhaust flames. The original photo is inscribed with a dedication to his parents.

fied by the achievement of five 'kills' – although he had, unusually, been awarded a DFC for a single night's action in which he had brought down two enemy aircraft. For most RAF fighter pilots, a DFC would have only been forthcoming after the achievement of at least five victories. Little wonder, then, that Richard felt he didn't deserve the award and considered that he had much to live up to.

Artistic interest in him was also attracted by Eric Kennington, a war artist engaged by the War Office. However, whether or not the interest was generated through Kennington's own keenness on him as a subject or if it was through the direction or commission of Kennington's wartime masters is not clear. What is clear, though, is that Kennington and Richard would go on to share a close but brief friendship. A friendship which Kennington himself would describe, after Richard's death, as an 'intimacy'. However, that friendship seems to have evolved much further on into the spring of 1941, although Kennington was inspired, through talking to Richard, to depict the dramatic scene of that first victory over Brentwood on 16 January, calling his work: 'Stevens' Rocket'.

'Stevens' Rocket' by Eric Kennington. The name for the work clearly alluded to the pioneering steam locomotive, 'Stephenson's Rocket'.

Finally, after some three weeks recovering from the ear injury, Pilot Officer Stevens was passed as fit to fly by a medical board on 6 February 1941. But this was not before he had been told, as he impatiently waited for his ear to heal, that if he pushed things too much, he could permanently damage his balance. "That's OK," he replied, "...I can fly just as well on my side."

The day after his medical board, Richard was back on the flight line at 15.10 hours for a 30-minute night-flying test in Hurricane V6934. The choice of that specific aircraft may well not have been a coincidence; after all, it was V6934 which had gone 'sick', along with himself, after the 16 January combat. Now, the old team were back. There was a war to be getting on with. Germans to bring down. And a DFC to be properly 'earned'.

Hurricane MkIIA B Flight 151 Sqn Wittering 1941 P.O. Stevens DSO. DFC.

Artist's impression of Pilot Officer Richard Stevens' 151 Squadron Hurricane, V6934.

Chapter Five

A PRINCE AMONG NIGHTFIGHTERS

For all his keenness to get back to operational flying, and despite two operational nightfighter patrols flown during the month, the amount of airtime available to Richard was severely restricted for the remainder of February 1941. Mostly, this was likely due to inclement weather conditions as much as anything else. Again, we turn to Flight Lieutenant Smith to explain how the meteorological conditions impacted on their fighter operations:

> "At this time, and generally throughout the war, all east coast airfields – including all the nightfighter stations – suffered not only from severe industrial pollution of the atmosphere, which resulted in a thick smog up to about 12,000 feet, but the airfields also suffered from low stratus creeping inland off the North Sea and giving very low cloud bases.

Eerily illuminated by a Chance light, a nightfighter Hurricane returns after another sortie.

"Also, there was no close fighter control of any kind for nightfighting. The ground control stations were used exclusively to aid the radar-equipped nightfighters. Thus, after a few hours on patrol, in complete darkness, and over smog, cloud or mist…well…there were very few pilots who knew exactly where they were. Stevens, though. He always knew. He always seemed to know exactly where he was.

"Again, there was the issue of maintaining control of the fighter because if an attempt was made to find the enemy, by banking and turning, the Hurricane's gyros would topple if 60 degrees of bank was exceeded. Thus, any blind-flying capability was lost. But it never seemed to bother Stevens."

Initially, the flights Richard made during February were all between the 7th and 11th of the month, with a break, then, until 22 February, and then just local night flying and a night-flying test on 27 and 28 February respectively. While frustrating for him, the weather had a part to play. Especially so considering the blizzard conditions which struck much of the eastern part of England between 18 and 22 February. Even more frustrating was the fact that if the weather conditions made it completely impossible to fly, that was not always the case for the Germans. Sometimes, their own bases were not being affected by the same weather patterns and the Luftwaffe's bombers could operate over Britain when conditions kept the defenders on the ground. The feeling of impotency, for Richard especially, must have been intense when these situations arose. However, as we shall see, weather conditions were not always a limiting factor for him.

If nothing else, though, the relatively quiet month must have helped with the further recuperation of his ear injury. At least, he wasn't put in a position where he might risk further damage to his weakened tympanic membrane by the excesses of extreme flight. That he might have viewed it that way, though, is unlikely. But March was set to be a slightly better hunting month.

As ever, much of the month was taken up with the almost endless round of night-flying tests, formation and practice attacks and sector 'recces'. After all, life on an operational squadron wasn't all about chasing the enemy all of the time. Indeed, even the apparently mundane crept into Richard's flying schedule for the month, and on 10 March he took up Defiant N3373 for a 25-minute flight with a Group Captain Dixon as his passenger on what was defined as a 'helmet test'. However, and despite the relative dearth of recent action, one of the other Wittering pilots, Flight Lieutenant Gareth Clayton, a Beaufighter pilot with 25 Squadron, recalled of Richard:

"He was an absolute one-off. You wouldn't come across people like that again. He was always at Wittering. He never went away. You could always count on him being in the air or haunting the ops room. He flew some astonishingly long hours in that Hurricane and was so fanatical about getting into the air that one night he came into the mess when we were fog bound and were just sat there twiddling our thumbs. He said: 'What the hell are you doing? Why don't you get into the air and do something?'"

It wasn't the first time that he had said just that, of course, but Clayton went on to explain that some pilots were natural nightfighter pilots, and others just weren't. Although he went on to have a distinguished and highly decorated career, Gareth Clayton was self-deprecating when it came to his own prowess in the role: "Whilst Stevens was a natural, a born nightfighter pilot, I wasn't. In fact, I managed to write off three of His Majesty's Beaufighters without even seeing a single German aircraft!"

Four days after his mundane 'helmet test' flight, though, in the early hours of 14 March, and back in Hurricane V6934 on a night-flying patrol, he found the enemy once again. However, we do know that Richard only took off after Wittering itself had been visited by a Luftwaffe raider and bombed, with some damage being caused to the airfield infrastructure. As the bombs were falling, he raced to his Hurricane – only to be told he couldn't take off because the runway lights were not lit. "I don't need bloody lights!" he retorted. "I'll get the bastard!", he shouted as he jumped onto the wing of the waiting Hurricane.

Albeit that the foregoing detail is omitted, his combat report takes up the story:

C Flight
151 Squadron
Attacked at 02.00, north of Aldeburgh.
Enemy aircraft at 15,000 feet. Junkers 88 claimed as probable.

P/O R P Stevens DFC (Ajax 61) 151 Squadron left Wittering in a Hurricane at 00.50 hours to intercept enemy aircraft. He was vectored near Raid M99 and sighted it flying east near Orford Ness at about 15,000 feet. The enemy aircraft was seen against the moon's reflection in the water being between the Hurricane and the moon. P/O Stevens was about 3,000 feet above and he immediately dived and made a quarter attack from 75 yards, hitting the fuselage, centre section and port motor. Return fire [was] seen from the top gun and afterwards from the bottom gun but was ineffective. The Ju 88 climbed steeply away leaving a white trail from its port engine. The Hurricane was unable to keep up with this as the constant speed unit would not go into fine pitch owing to freezing, but a final burst was fired from about 150/200 yards and hits observed on fuselage before enemy aircraft climbed out of range. The glycol trail was followed up but was eventually lost, last

RAF Wittering during the spring of 1941. The main A1 road runs past the camp on the right. Damage from one of the Luftwaffe bombing attacks can be seen to the roof of one of the hangars.

seen going in a downward direction, easterly. It is considered that with one engine damaged the enemy aircraft would have difficulty in returning to base. P/O Stevens was about 25 miles east of Orford Ness and he returned to base and landed at about 02.55 hours. Visibility very good. Full moon. No cloud. Fifty rounds fired from each gun. No stoppages. R/T satisfactory. Reflector sight used fully dimmed. Pilot wishes to stress interception due to good vectoring and no contrail at all. He also considers that the Hurricane is hardly fast enough.

While the apparent escape of the Ju 88 must have been frustrating, it at least went to show that there was still potential 'trade' out there for hunters like Richard. Whether his 'probable' claim is related or not, it is difficult to say, although a Junkers 88 of III./KG51 did make an emergency landing that night at Trouville returning from operations over Britain. Additionally, Uffz Peter Stahl, a Junkers 88 pilot with II./KG30, later wrote of a sortie that night which may well tie in to Richard's interception. Having spotted a nightfighter, he reacted instinctively:

"Without further ado, I pulled Cäsar (his Ju 88) into a steep half-roll to port and let it fall upside down into the night. Surely, nobody could follow that! I had just levelled off when Hein comes over the intercom again repeating his warning. The devil! Once more, we shoot like a stone into the blackness below. And then a third time!"

Certainly, there are elements about Stahl's description making it very tempting to link Richard with this episode, although that can only remain as speculation. What is certain, though, is that the Junkers 88 was a fast and nimble aircraft, and in the right hands it could perform upwards rolls, unladen, and in a fast dive could often outrun all RAF fighters of the day. On this occasion, of course, Richard had complained the Hurricane was 'hardly fast enough'. That, though, might largely be associated with problems he had experienced that night with the operation of his propeller's constant speed unit. It was certainly an episode which frustrated the ever impatient and impetuous Stevens, who wanted to even the score of Wittering's bombing attack with a confirmed 'kill'!

At around this time, George Young was deputy airfield flying control officer at Wittering and he recalled Richard being told: "You can't fly tonight, the weather is too bad." Young went on to explain:

"It didn't worry him a bit. I recall being advised that he was taking off and I recall him coming over the R/T and just saying: 'Airborne'. And that was it. From then on, he didn't need any help at all for the simple reason he just wouldn't answer when called up on the R/T. Quite often, and when I couldn't get our hero to answer, the senior controller would take the headset and call him saying: 'This is Squadron Leader so-and-so, will you answer at once.' He never did. Once, the station commander Group Captain Basil Embry tried to contact him, saying: "This is the station commander..." But to no avail. I think he got into trouble that time, but just smiled and claimed the mic and headphones in his helmet weren't working. [Note: it is possible that the 'flying helmet test' on 10 March was related to this incident! Author.] Often, he'd be given a vector towards a target but he wouldn't answer and just went off and did his own thing where he thought he'd find Germans. And he usually did. Sometimes, we just couldn't get him down, but eventually he would come home in the morning, just as light was breaking, having shot down German aircraft anywhere between London, Birmingham or Hull."

Being his 'own man', and one who was minded to have as little truck as absolutely necessary with military discipline, Richard was inevitably going to come up against authority on occasion. And that certainly was the case at Wittering. Quite apart from the excuse of communications difficulties, there was at least one other occasion when it is said that he was in deep water with the station's disciplinary officer for some unknown misdemeanour according to members of 151 Squadron ground crew. His punishment,

Cyril Mead (right) was Richard Stevens' fitter on 151 Squadron and is seen here with LAC Cloke, the rigger, along with one of the squadron's Hurricanes. The photo would have been taken before 151 Squadron's transition to nightfighting as evidenced by the day camouflage scheme.

they recalled, was to be confined to camp whilst he dug out a defensive machine-gun post on the hedge of Wittering's perimeter, and Cyril Mead recalled seeing him in overalls and setting to digging a trench and emplacement overlooking the A1 road which skirted the east side of the airfield. Part of the defensive position went underneath the hedge, and while it is said that Richard evidently didn't object to the menial punishment handed down to him, he did object to being 'confined to camp' – albeit that he spent most of his time there, anyway. As a result, Cyril Mead said, part of Richard's defensive position involved him digging out a tunnel which ran under the hedge to the side of the main road, and through which he wriggled his escape to walk boldly into nearby Stamford. The tunnel, according to the legend handed down, evidently served a useful purpose for Richard Stevens during the period of his confinement. However, is this another mythical tale?

Flight Lieutenant I S 'Black' Smith thinks so:

> "I have never heard of an officer being confined to camp unless he was under 'open' or 'close' arrest while undergoing or awaiting Courts Martial. Which Stevens never was. 'Confinement to camp' is a degree of punishment and a formal term which applies only to airmen below the rank of corporal. Thus,

the story that 'Steve' was ever confined to camp must be fictitious. Also a fiction is the story of the trench through the hedge. And I would have heard about these things. There was no need for him to use such an exit as there was never any restriction on officers leaving via one of the two guarded gates. And an officer would never have been given this sort of punishment, anyway."

Whatever the truth of the matter, it is yet another tale about Richard Stevens which has endured and is widely repeated in many references to him. And there can be no doubting his bullish and contemptuous attitude towards authority. As his brother, James, later recalled:

"He was totally bloody-minded. Tactless and determined, and sure – perhaps too sure – of his own technical ability to cope with any situation as well as being totally at odds with any rules and regulations which offended his common sense."

As the month drew to a close, and somewhat to his chagrin, Richard found himself flying five sorties in Defiant N3403 with a Sergeant Lammin in the turret. Of the Defiant, Richard's brother, James, later recalled: "He regarded the aircraft with complete and total contempt."

Variously, the Defiant sorties were sector recce, local formation flying, a night-flying test and then a transit flight to RAF Coltishall. But, as we have seen, flying and fighting in the Defiant was not for Richard and, as April beckoned, so did some better hunting success. He was about to properly get into his stride, across a period of his nightfighting prowess which would later result in Group Captain William Helmore, in one of his regular BBC broadcasts about the work of the RAF, referring to him as '...that prince amongst nightfighters'. Indeed, that 'prince' was about to embark on a series of successes, which, in Richard's own view, would have seen his DFC as properly earned.

The next successful night interception would see yet another double victory on 9 April. Again, we must turn to the combat report for the story:

P/O R P Stevens DFC, 'Steeple 3', left Wittering at 00.52 hours in a Hurricane with orders to orbit Coventry on 'Fighter Night' operations. At about 01.14 hours when at 19,000 feet over Coventry he sighted a He 111 flying westerly below him, against cloud layer. P/O Stevens dived and closed to 75 yards making a quarter attack at 15,000 feet and hit the belly of enemy aircraft. A large explosion followed (seen also by Flight Lieutenant [illegible]) and the aircraft dived. The port motor was alight, and another burst into the centre section and fuselage caused flames to break out. The enemy aircraft was twisting and diving in a southerly direction and entered the cloud layer at about 5,000 feet. P/O Stevens followed and saw the enemy aircraft blazing ahead of him and with bombs and incendiaries blowing up. It eventually crashed and exploded in a mass of flames. The Hurricane then resumed patrol and climbed to 12,000 feet and orbited [illegible]. At about 01.42 hours P/O Stevens sighted another He 111 about 1,000 feet above him and also travelling Westerly. He tailed this and at about 200 yards range the enemy started firing from the lower gun position. The Hurricane dived, came up underneath, and fired a deflection burst from about 100 yards at nose and centre section. To evade return fire from the lower gun, P/O Stevens pulled up sharply on the port side and gave another burst upon which the enemy gunner ceased fire. The top gunner of the enemy aircraft was firing accurately, and the Hurricane was hit several times. P/O Stevens made another quarter attack from below and saw starboard motor on fire and leaving a stream of glycol which obscured his windscreen. He dropped back to wipe the windscreen with his glove and returned to the attack and noticed the port motor on fire. A further burst from astern and below from 100 yards caused bits of the enemy aircraft to fall away and it then dived steeply into cloud layer. A further burst was fired and hit the enemy aircraft which was not seen again although P/O Stevens followed it through the cloud. When last seen, both motors were on fire and the inside of the fuselage was also burning.

P/O Stevens then returned to base and landed at 01.53 hours.

There was no failure of equipment. Reflector sight was used fully dimmed.

Slipstream effect was experienced. R/T was satisfactory. One gun stopped through faulty round, but otherwise all ammunition was fired except 28 rounds in each of the other seven guns.

In many ways, combat reports like this one – so typical of those filed for Pilot Officer Stevens – rather belie the true nature of the drama they unfold. Almost matter of fact in their telling. But there was nothing matter of fact about this combat, or any other. However, this report perhaps deserves more scrutiny than others and for a number of reasons.

First, Richard makes reference to a 'Fighter Night' and it is important to explain what such an operation actually was. Its definition was succinctly set out by Marshal of the Royal Air Force Sir Sholto Douglas:

> "Perhaps the most remarkable feature of this night's operations [He was writing, here, of 10 April 1941. Author] was the success of the Hurricane and Spitfire flying in the Bomber Stream. On various other nights in April and May, aircraft on 'Fighter Night' patrols, claimed the destruction of 20 enemy aircraft in the aggregate. The impression that 'Fighter Nights' was an unprofitable operation is widespread, but these figures show that, given good weather, moonlight, and a substantial concentration of enemy aircraft, these patrols could achieve satisfactory results. It was, however, only at periods when the moon was above the horizon that any success was achieved.
>
> "Operation 'Fighter Night' was, of course, always regarded with disfavour by the A.A. gunners, whose chances of success it diminished. When it was first put into effect, the guns in the target area were forbidden to fire; but it was argued that their silence might cause apprehension amongst the public, and later they were allowed to fire up to heights safely below that of the lowest fighters. Such a restriction of A.A. fire was only justified, of course, when the conditions were particularly favourable to fighters, but the figures just quoted show that in these conditions its justification was beyond dispute. It is interesting to note that, despite the limitation imposed on them, the guns in the target area were not always barren of success on these occasions. While generally the guns kept the German bombers up to the heights at which the fighters could most conveniently engage them, it would seem that on occasions the fighters must have forced individual bombers down into the A.A. belt."

Very largely, the RAF fighters engaged on 'Fighter Night' patrols were those operating in the dayfighter role but seconded to night-time operations to bolster defences. However, 151 Squadron was already operating in the nightfighter role, anyway. Most of the other day squadron fighters who were allocated 'Fighter Night' operations had limited success, though. For one thing, many otherwise experienced pilots found that flying Spitfires or Hurricanes at night was less than ideal. For one thing, the glare from the exhaust ports (invisible in daylight) could seriously impair night vision, and to an extent this was even if glare baffles were fitted. For Richard, though, none of these issues presented him with anything of a problem. But that didn't mean that he didn't have to prepare his already exceptional night vision for night ops. In fact, he spent some time sitting in the dispersal hut in darkness before venturing to his Hurricane to fly. And woe betide any 'Erk' who hadn't turned off or dimmed any illumination in the cockpit. To him, lights at night were an anathema and even the already dim lamp of the Barr & Stroud reflector gunsight was always noted as used 'fully dimmed'. Sometimes, he didn't even use the reflector sight at all but just relied on the bead sight mounted ahead of the cockpit.

In terms of sighting, it is also important to consider a number of aspects apart from the darkness. For one thing, and despite the terseness of Richard's combat reports, it is important to remember that the German bombers he engaged could be flying in any direction at any height from ground level up to the bomber's operational ceiling at, say, five miles a minute. Its pilot could dive, climb, jink and alter height and direction and the aircraft would never be still for even a fraction of a second. If the enemy pilot is flying straight ahead, the aircraft travels 130 yards in a second and while he cannot climb at the same rate, he can dive at 390 feet in one second and during that dive he could also alter direction and position at a rate of 130 yards a second. The nightfighter pilot, then, has to fly into a vast blackness and intercept an aircraft that is able to move about in the parameters described. Not only that, but the pilot could vary the aircraft's speed between maximum and minimum; at one second, the enemy aircraft could be around 30,000 ft high and 45 seconds later it could have dived down rapidly to a much lower altitude. Additionally, the nightfighter pilot must be able to see the enemy before he can destroy him. These difficulties, then, go some way towards explaining why fighter pilots like Richard were very much in the minority. And why he was so exceptional. Indeed, in his combat report of 9 April 1941 he talks of: "The enemy aircraft...twisting and diving in a southerly direction and [entering] the cloud layer at about 5,000 feet." This sentence cannot possibly convey the actuality of the events described, where the aircraft dived rapidly, twisting and turning, from 15,000 ft to 5,000 ft in moments. And, throughout all of that, he stuck with his quarry before solving and then executing the sighting equation. Little wonder, then, that the noted RAF commentator would describe him, after his death, as a 'prince among nightfighters'.

In order to improve his chances, we also know that Richard flew with his cockpit open. This afforded him marginally better vision – especially to each side, if not ahead. Gone were any distortions from the Perspex panels or any interruptions in his field of vision caused by the canopy framing. And, on 9 July, he almost certainly had his canopy open during the engagement. In the body of his report he talks of having to clean glycol from his windscreen using his glove. This was not glycol on the outside of the screen, but on the inside where it had been drawn by the strange effects of airflow. Cold and exhaust fumes were also a challenge, but one Luftwaffe air gunner who came up against him described what it was like encountering the 'Lone Wolf' at night:

> "We were flying very slowly at under 100 feet in misty conditions and I thought we were invisible. Suddenly, I looked up and saw the shadow of a nightfighter right on top of us. I just couldn't believe it as the cockpit and propeller slowly moved inside our tail plane. When he opened up with his cannon I thought he had collided with us because our debris was all over

One German aircrew member, after being attacked by Richard Stevens, reported "...a black helmeted figure silhouetted in the open cockpit". Echoing that scenario is Eric Kennington's painting, 'Readiness', intended to represent Richard in his open cockpit.

him, but there, quite clearly to be seen against the background glare of our burning aircraft, was a black-helmeted figure, quite clearly silhouetted in the open cockpit."

Again, here is reality; the real-life drama as opposed to the clinical and factual detail of the combat reports. Of those reports, too, it is interesting to note that all are written by a third party (presumably the squadron intelligence officer) rather than in the first person as was mostly the case across RAF Fighter Command. Nothing can be particularly read into this, other than the fact that it was clearly just this squadron's way of doing things.

But what of the two Heinkels which Pilot Officer Richard Stevens had so surgically excised from the sky that night?

The first of the two bombers was a Heinkel He 111 H-5 of 2./KG27 (W.Nr 4018) which was sent flaming into the ground at Little Hill Farm, Wellesbourne, Warwickshire, at around 01.15 hours. Of the crew (coincidentally, four of them having the same surname), three baled out into captivity; Ofw H Müller, Fw H Müller and Fw G Schäfer being taken POW. Meanwhile, Oblt G Müller died when his parachute failed to open and Sd Fr W-D Müller was found dead in the wreckage. Given the ferocity of the attack, the fusillade hitting the bomber and the on-board explosions it is truly remarkable that any of the crew survived. However, if the survival of three men from the Wellesbourne Heinkel was remarkable, then the survival of another two German airmen in the second aircraft destroyed that night was miraculous.

The second aircraft, a Heinkel 111 of 3./KG55, crashed at Roes Rest Farm, Peckleton, Leicestershire, and photographs of the smashed-up wreckage illustrate just how unlikely it seems that anybody might have lived through such a violent crash. However, and having read Richard's factual account of the shoot-down, let us leave it to one of the lucky survivors of that second Heinkel, Fw Hans Kaufold, to tell the story in his own words of his lucky escape after that fateful encounter with Pilot Officer R P Stevens:

> "Our crew, Hptm Otto Bodemeyer, Ofw Heinz Söllner, Fw Herbert Link and I crossed the coast in clear bright moonlight at Portsmouth at 4,000 feet, where we were shot at by Flak, and then over Coventry we were attacked and shot down by a Spitfire [sic] night hunter; this was approximately between 3.30 and 4.00 hours [NB: the Germans were operating on Central European Time, hence the apparent disparity in timings]. The fighter just came out of the darkness at us. It then attacked again, but we could not fight back. The attacker was in a good position, and in the first attack Link, the flight engineer, was badly wounded in his upper arm. Our 'plane burnt rather quickly after that, and the intercom had also failed so we were therefore

Wreckage of the Heinkel 111 H-5 of 2./KG27 brought down by Richard at Little Hill Farm, Wellesbourne, on 9 April 1941.

Feldwebel Hans Kaufold in the gondola of his Heinkel.

Kaufold (on the fuselage) poses with a colleague and a 3./KG55 Heinkel 111.

unable to communicate. The last thing I heard was someone shouting to our pilot: 'Söllner! There are clouds at 1,000 metres. Let's hide there!'

"Then, due to a misunderstanding – and not being able to hear anything

Kaufold's Heinkel 111 is readied for another sortie as 50 kg and 250 kg bombs are prepared for loading.

because of the broken intercom – I realised that Bodemeyer and Söllner had already baled out and we were alone in the aircraft. Herbert had lost a lot of blood, and he was now unconscious. We were already down below 1,000 metres, and the 'plane was well alight. I cannot describe what really happened next, as I too went unconscious. The next thing I knew, the 'plane had crashed, and I was lying in a field or meadow with my flying suit on fire. I can only think that Link and I had been catapulted out.

"There was a house nearby, but I couldn't see very much because it was dark. I managed to walk away from the burning 'plane along a country lane and was able to avoid a man coming towards me. When I reached a main road, I sat down in a ditch because my leg hurt. By now, things were getting quite lively. A fire engine and a number of cars went past me to the burning Heinkel, and I could hear voices and the sound of dogs barking. And I could hear what I thought were gunshots. This worried me a bit, until I realised it was the sound of ammunition exploding in the flames of our blazing Heinkel. From the other noises I could hear, though, they were obviously out looking for me. I wondered what I should do, so in the end I decided to boldly march off down the road – but it was more of a limp because of my injured leg. Suddenly, a car came around a bend in the road and stopped just in front of me. Out got an RAF officer with a pistol, which he pointed at me, and shouted 'Hands up!' For me, the war was over."

For a young lad called John Pratley, however, it was a night of excitement at his home in nearby Thelsford Cottage when he was woken by his father who rushed into his bedroom shouting: "Come and see a German bomber on fire!" (See page 13.) A night he would never forget.

Top: Wreckage of the Heinkel 111 at Roes Rest Farm, Peckleton. Bottom: The tail of the Roes Rest Farm Heinkel was acquired by 151 Squadron as a trophy and is seen here with the 151 Squadron badge and motto painted onto the rudder by Richard.

Chapter Six

WITTERING'S DRAGON

The next success in what was to be a run of good fortune was to occur the very next night on 10/11 April 1941, Good Friday, and during a period when the night Blitz was in full swing. The relevant combat report outlines events for us:

> **B Flight**
> 151 Squadron
> Attacked 23.43, north-east of Banbury.
> Enemy aircraft at 16,000 feet. He 111 claimed as destroyed.
>
> P/O Stevens left Wittering at 22.44 with orders to patrol Birmingham in Hurricane 'Steeple 43' at 23.43. Enemy aircraft sighted ten miles north-east of Banbury at 16,000 feet flying south. Attacking from astern, lumps of the enemy aircraft flew off and the Hurricane was covered in oil. No return fire. The enemy aircraft dived vertically but a further burst was fired from astern before the aircraft crashed in a field which was covered in burning wreckage. 1,600 rounds were fired. No stoppages. R/T good. Cloudy with nearly full moon. Landed at Wittering at 00.24.

This time, his victim was actually a Junkers 88 and not the He 111 provisionally identified by Richard in his report. The aircraft, a machine of II./KG1, fell at Murcott, Oxfordshire, killing the four crew members, Fw W John, Fw J Berger, Uffz E Sadegor and Uffz H Schmid.

After landing back at Wittering, and having re-fuelled and re-armed and having had the smeared German oil cleaned from his Hurricane's wings, fuselage and cockpit canopy, Richard was again ready for the off shortly after 2 a.m. This time, it was set to be a repeat of his first double success on the night of 16 January, three months earlier, when he again crept up on an unsuspecting raider in the very early hours of the morning:

> "He 111 Attacked at 02.29, between Kettering and Thrapston at

18,000 feet.

P/O Stevens left with a Hurricane, 'Steeple 43', for a freelance patrol at 02.15. At approx. 02.29 an He 111 was sighted flying east at 1,000 feet above P/O Stevens. He closed to 200 yards and then swung slightly to port and fired a short burst at 150 yards. The whole burst hit, and Stevens was temporarily blinded. Something blew up in the enemy aircraft and P/O Stevens dropped back until the fuselage shadow filled the sight ring. Taking careful aim, he fired a second burst and large lumps flew off the enemy aircraft. No return fire. Swung to starboard and noted starboard motor alight and fuselage burning inside. The enemy aircraft turned slowly over and went into a steep dive. Seen to hit the ground and break into pieces. P/O Stevens continued the patrol but with no further intercepts. Getting misty. Landed at 05.30 hours."

This time, there was no faulting Richard's identification. The aircraft, a Heinkel 111 P-2 of 9./KG55 (G1 + AT, W.Nr 2827) fell to earth at Rothwell Lodge, Kettering. Remarkably, and despite the absolutely withering hail of gunfire, an on-board explosion and a fire seen inside the fuselage, two of the crew managed to escape by parachute. Of these, Ltn G Buse was taken POW along with Fw W Kanera, although the latter died in captivity on 5 June 1942. Uffz K Roick, Uffz F Schober and Fw W Schelle were all killed – most probably in the terrific fusillade of cannon fire, or else sufficiently incapacitated by the attack that they were unable to escape the stricken bomber. After taking such enormous punishment, the aircraft lost height rapidly and narrowly missed a farm building before careering across a field alongside the A6 road, the disintegrating wreckage burning fiercely. A short while afterwards, another German aircraft dropped bombs near the flaming wreckage, although whether this was a deliberate act or merely coincidental remains unknown. Despite the almost total destruction of the airframe, however, RAF air intelligence investigators found no less than 30 .303 bullet strikes in what was

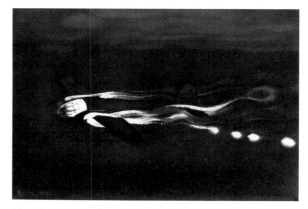

This Kennington depiction of another Richard Stevens' night 'kill' might well have reflected Richard's description of the interception on 10/11 April 1941 when he described "[the] starboard motor alight and fuselage burning inside".

*An artist's representation of the view from Richard's cock-
pit of his interception of the Heinkel 111 which he shot
down over Kettering on the night of 10/11 April 1941 –
another occasion when Richard achieved a double victory
in a single night.*

left of the bomber.

Such was the horror of the night for Günther Buse, however, that when he was contacted by Terry Thompson during the period of his research work for this book, Günther replied politely but firmly. He simply wrote:

"You ask for details of the circumstances surrounding how my crew and I were shot down. I have been asked for help with this before, but I am afraid that I cannot help you. The incident still upsets me to this day. I ask for your understanding in this. Sincerely, G Buse."

In all probability, he was continuing to suffer from what we would today call Post Traumatic Stress Disorder, or PTSD. It was, of course, the case that so many of those who survived such events in wartime would suffer similarly. For Ltn Buse and his surviving crew member it had been a night of sheer horror.

With Richard now getting back into his stride, as it were, he had to wait until towards the end of that month, however, before another target presented itself to him. Meanwhile, he continued to practise and hone his combat and night-flying skills, mug up on aircraft recognition and air-to-air gunnery and to organise the painting of what was a dramatic emblem on the starboard engine cowling of his regular Hurricane, V6934. The artwork comprised a fire-breathing demonic dragon, an RAF ensign held in its tail and viciously spearing a Nazi bird of prey with a trident. As the often restrained and frequently understated nose art of the period went, it was certainly extremely flamboyant. And it surely reflected the unusual nature of the man who was Richard Playne Stevens. He also painted an enigmatic red question mark on the port engine cowling of the same Hurricane. It would seem, too, that at one time or another a Hurricane he flew sported another slightly more cheeky emblem on its cowling, as his sister Helen recalled:

"Once, he somehow managed to contrive a landing at Penshurst aerodrome which wasn't very far from our home near Tunbridge Wells and we went across to see him. I don't know if it was by prior arrangement, or what, but there was this menacing black Hurricane. He showed us around it, but he told me not to look at the other side. Intrigued, I ducked under the engine to look

This somewhat garish and surreal emblem was painted onto the starboard engine cowling panel of Richard Stevens' Hurricane by Richard himself. Its style reflects the work done by Richard on the wall murals in Palestine when he served in the Palestine Police.

anyway. Well, you would, wouldn't you? There, on the side of the engine was chalked, not painted, well, a very rude but very well executed (if I may say so!) school-boyish picture. A phallic one, in fact. Underneath, it said: "Dirty Dick".[3] It all seemed a bit incongruous and childish, given the deadly purpose of the Hurricane. Anyway, I think I blushed, but Dick said: 'Well, I did tell you not to look!' However, things such as this didn't faze us in the Stevens family. We were all pretty much open-minded and really not at all prudish in any way. But I'm surprised he got away with it in the RAF – maybe that is why it was chalked? So that he could quickly rub it off if he had to.'"

It wasn't long before Richard was eventually able to spear yet another Nazi bird of prey, the main text of the relevant combat report for 20 April again relating the night's events:

> P/O Stevens left Wittering as 'Steeple 43' at 03.28 hours. Vec-
> tored 165° to approx. position of enemy aircraft and then orbited.
> At 04.11 hours he sighted, north-east of London by means of Ack

---

3   The chalked name, 'Dirty Dick', was perhaps a reference harking back to his unhappy days at Hurstpierpoint College and thumbing his nose at those experiences. Also, during a visit to see his former Wrightways colleagues at Ringway, Manchester, during mid-1941, George Wainwright recalled Richard arriving in his all-black Hurricane which had a half moon emblem painted on the engine cowling.

Richard's sister Helen.

Ack fire, a He 111 flying west at 10,000 feet. The enemy aircraft was 3-400 feet above and on the port side, travelling slowly.

He closed carefully, avoided detection and opened fire in a quarter attack at 150 yards range from port, repeating this from the other side and finally a stern attack.

Return fire from the top gunner was experienced. This was avoided by side slipping beneath the enemy aircraft. The enemy aircraft was weaving and changing altitude. P/O Stevens concentrated on the port engine which blew up. 'One more burst for luck' was fired as the enemy aircraft went down trailing black and white smoke. As the enemy aircraft was preparing to 'land' east of Chatham, P/O Stevens, with the aid of the Chatham searchlights, 'assisted' in its landing.

For most nightfighter pilots, British anti-aircraft fire was considered a menace and a dangerous one. For Richard, they were pointers as to where enemy aircraft might be found and he regularly flew towards or through a barrage looking for prey.

In his report, we see the master tactician at work – avoiding detection and closing carefully. Perhaps, in his nocturnal hunting, Richard was sometimes mindful of a sentence in T E Lawrence's *Seven Pillars of Wisdom*: "Nine-tenths of tactics are certain and taught in books: but the irrational tenth is like the kingfisher flashing across the pool, and that is the test of generals."

During this engagement, the aircraft was a Heinkel 111 H-5 of 7./KG4 which did indeed attempt to make a forced landing after the attack, finally coming down at 04.30 hours at Whipstakes Meadow, Stockbury, Kent, and breaking in two after it skidded across a field before striking an embankment. Of the crew, Oblt J Baierl and Gefr W Mrozeck were lucky to be captured, albeit wounded, but Uffz G Schumann and Oberfw T Völker both lost their lives. The cryptic comments regarding the 'assistance' given the Heinkel's landing is taken to mean anything but assistance, but rather that the searchlights and Stevens, between them, conspired to hinder its landing. In this endeavour they seem to have succeeded.

That the Heinkel was reported as 'flying slowly' might well have had some significance in terms of Luftwaffe night operations at that time, which was becoming an increasingly dangerous one for bombers flying over Britain as nightfighter defences were finally coming into their own. Generally, speed was of the essence for the Luftwaffe raiders as it limited their time in hostile skies and consequently reduced the period of time they were at risk. But it was not always so. In fact, in one recorded instance, a Heinkel 111 was flying barely above the stall while an attacking Beaufighter pilot throttled right back but was unable to stay behind it. This, of course, only worked on very dark nights with minimal visual distance, otherwise the bomber would be a sitting duck. Such as on the night of 20 April, which saw RAF Fighter Command launch a total of 101 sorties on dusk, night and dawn patrols in severely unfavourable weather. Of these 101 sorties, only one fighter pilot claimed success; Pilot Officer R P Stevens had found Oblt Baierl's Heinkel, flying slowly to thwart any fighter attack. But Baierl and his crew had not reckoned on Richard and his night-time prowess.

In his hunting, he used not only his exceptional night vision but also looked for anti-aircraft bursts, often flying right into a barrage because he knew it to be the likely place where he would find the enemy. The moon, too, was a valuable asset with aircraft sometimes silhouetted against moonlit reflections on the sea, or else showing up in its luminescence. For this reason, too, some canny Luftwaffe pilots – if they were able – would deliberately fly detours to keep the moon at an angle and to one side and reduce the risk of detection. For instance, flying directly towards the moon would place the bomber in a position to a stalking nightfighter's advantage. But, however canny the Luftwaffe crews, it was fair to say that Richard had learned all the tricks and knew, for instance, that the bombers would often fly just above or just below the cloud base. That way, the bomber could quickly slip into cloud cover in the event of trouble. The tricks of the trade had to be learned by attacker and defender alike.

Whatever their tricks, and however clever the guile, though, the bald statistics were getting increasingly worrisome for Luftwaffe bomber crews. For example, losses to German bombers in January 1941 were standing at a mere 0.02%, with three bombers shot down this way. Of these, of course, two were claimed by none other than Pilot Officer R P Stevens. By May of 1941, though, the losses of Luftwaffe bombers to night-fighters had risen to 3.93%, representing a total of 96 bombers shot down by night-fighters. In terms of this 3.93%, Richard himself was helping to rack up the collective score as well as his own.

With his tally rising, Pilot Officer Stevens must have begun to feel at last that he had justifiably earned some credit for that DFC – or was at least earning it. Now, however, came another announcement in the *London Gazette* on 29 April, little more than a week after he had downed the Heinkel at Stockbury. The citation for a Bar to his DFC read:

> "This officer has done particularly outstanding work with his squadron on night operations and has on three occasions shot down two enemy aircraft in one night. Pilot Officer Stevens shows a great determination to attack the enemy and is prepared to fly under the most difficult weather conditions. His courage, determination, thoroughness and skill have set an excellent example to his unit."

Now, his 'kill' score was mounting, his medal tally increasing and press interest in 'Cat's Eyes Stevens' rising, too. However, Richard's success when flying from RAF Wittering was tempered by another series of night-time air attacks on the airfield by the Luftwaffe. "It was as if the bloody Germans knew where Stevens was operating from and were out to get him," said Cyril Mead, his fitter. "And I wasn't the only one at Wittering who thought it!", he added. The most serious raid was that carried out on the night of 8 May 1941, with 151 Squadron's operations record book noting the tragic facts:

> "Our efforts were curtailed by a Ju 88 which dropped a stick of eight anti-personnel bombs across 'A' Flight dispersal, writing off two aircraft and damaging four others also killing F/O Carlin – he was the only casualty – his loss is felt by all. A standing patrol was carried out by 'B' Flight for the rest of the night over the aerodrome."

Then, in a final sentence and almost bearing out Cyril Mead's suspicions, the record book adds: "We were bombed again."

The casualty in that attack was, in fact, Flying Officer Sydney Carlin MC, DFC, DCM, a Defiant air gunner with 151 Squadron and a man who had a story every bit as remarkable and unusual as Richard's. Not only that, he was an astonishing 52 years of age and yet he was still flying operationally and making Richard far from the eldest man on the squadron! Carlin, who was known as 'Timbertoes' – a nickname on account of his wooden leg gained when he lost a leg through wounds in the First World War – had had the most remarkable of military careers; variously, lance corporal cavalryman (where he earned a DCM), later commissioned and earning an MC in an action which cost him his leg and, later, an immediate DFC after he had joined the RFC to become a pilot, in which role he had served both with success and distinction despite his disability.

Briefly, on the outbreak of the Second World War, Carlin was commissioned in the army as an officer in a Royal Artillery anti-aircraft unit in Malta before re-mustering in the RAF and training as an air gunner, in time to participate in the Battle of Britain on Defiants of 264 Squadron. At Wittering, and as was his entitlement, he caused amusement by variously wearing tunics sporting either a pilot's or air gun-

Flying Officer Sydney 'Timbertoes' Carlin MC, DFC, DCM, was a First World War veteran who flew as a Defiant air gunner with 151 Squadron and was killed in the German air attack at RAF Wittering on 8 May 1941. In this photograph he is seen during his earlier service with 264 Squadron during the Battle of Britain.

ner's brevet. All told, he was an exceptional man and an interesting character. Little wonder, then, that the 151 Squadron operations record books said of him: "His loss is felt by all." What it does not tell, though, is how he died.

When the bombs started falling, Carlin didn't take cover and instead he cycled furiously to a parked Defiant at dispersal. Here, he was climbing into his turret with its four power-operated .303 Browning machine guns when the bombs detonated nearby. His intention was to engage the enemy aircraft from his turret while still on the ground. Unfortunately, the heroic Syd was caught in the blast when two of the squadron's aircraft were destroyed and four others badly damaged. In the blast, his arm was blown off, but when the raid was over and people rushed to help him, Timbertoes was already dead. It must be said that 151 Squadron certainly had its share of 'characters' across the period of the 1941 Blitz.

On the following two nights, Wittering was yet again bombed. But, at last, Richard would wreak some havoc again and get some vengeance for the bombings and for Carlin's death. If not vengeance on the actual raiders themselves, then at least on the Luftwaffe as a general entity. Further scores just added to the British press's fascination with him and the next two claims – again, achieved as a double victory – would come during the early hours of the night of 9 May. By now, combat reports like this were getting more and more routine for Pilot Officer R P Stevens, DFC & Bar:

> P/O Stevens left Wittering at 01.12 hours on a freelance patrol in a Hurricane I (8 x machine guns). AA fire at Grantham attracted his attention and at 01.41 he sighted a He 111 silhouetted in searchlights at approx. 10,000 feet. P/O Stevens climbed from 4,000 feet to intercept but failed. Permission was obtained by S/L Adams (OIC 151 Squadron) for him to investigate fire to the north. He proceeded to search the Hull area and about 02.20 saw a He 111 at 9,000 feet passing 2,000 feet below him. He dived and closed to 200 yards. P/O Stevens made a fine quarter attack and large flashes were seen in the fuselage. After a further similar attack, oil and glycol came from the starboard motor and covered the Hurricane. Cleaned windscreen using the glycol pump. There was no return fire, but the enemy aircraft took evasive action consisting of violent S turns. Following a final attack from astern and below, the enemy aircraft turned over and dived into cloud.
>
> P/O Stevens resumed the patrol and five minutes later a He 111 was sighted flying east from Hull at 7,000 feet and 2,000 feet above cloud. Pulling the plug, P/O Stevens caught it as it dived for cloud cover and attacked from starboard quarter and slightly above. Approx. range 250/150 yards. The port motor of the enemy aircraft blew up in a shower of sparks and large pieces flew off while the enemy aircraft disappeared. No return fire - continued patrol with no further success until the main tanks were empty. Landed at 03.33. (P/O Stevens thinks both enemy aircraft came down in the sea.)4
>
> 1,200 rounds fired. Weather good but cloud layer between 400/600 (tops). Visibility excellent. Speed of enemy aircraft 180/200 mph except the second enemy aircraft which was much faster.

When he landed at Wittering, just as the first rays of sun were lighting up the morning sky, the Hurricane's engine coughed and spluttered as he came in over the boundary marker, the aircraft rolling to a premature halt. As detailed in the combat report, both of the fuel tanks were literally empty. The aircraft had almost been running on the proverbial fumes on its final approach across the main A1, The Great North Road.

---

4   Attached to this combat report at The National Archives was a copy of a telegram to RAF Fighter Command's 12 Group HQ, instructing that this statement in brackets should be deleted from the report.

A Junkers 88 of KG54 readies for another sortie. Richard often encountered this nimble bomber, shooting down at least five of them. On the night of 9 May 1941, aircraft of this unit were operating over Hull when Richard claimed two Heinkel 111 bombers in another double victory.

That night had seen a very heavy attack on Hull involving 120 bombers and it had been the fires of a burning city and flak bursts associated with the raid that had attracted Richard's attention from a distance. With Hull out of Wittering's sector and operational area of responsibility, and in the Church Fenton and Catterick sectors, Squadron Leader Adams, the commanding officer of 151 Squadron, had sought and obtained permission for Richard to venture north. Attracted like a moth to a candle flame, he had homed in on the fires and flak explosions and where he knew the enemy would be. Yet again, it had been a double victory in one night and although the identity of his two victims remains unknown, III./KG40, I./KG27, II./KG55 and II./KG54 all lost aircraft during the Hull raid. However, no wrecks on land can be associated with Richard's claims and so it must be assumed, as he had concluded, that the aircraft came down in the sea. Either way, the two claims were granted as confirmed victories.

On the following night, and frustrated yet again, he failed to find any German bombers – albeit that it was one of the heaviest night raids of the entire Blitz. On which the C-in-C Fighter Command, Marshal of the RAF Sir Sholto Douglas, GCB, MC, DFC would later write:

> "On the night of 10th May the enemy made the most ambitious attack on London that he had attempted up to that time, or indeed was ever to at-

tempt. Although contemporary estimates were lower, it is now known that the German bomber force flew more than 500 sorties on this night. Visibility was good and the results were eminently satisfactory. A total of 60 single-engine fighters were sent to patrol at various heights over London, 20 over Beachy Head, and smaller numbers over the other approaches to the capital, while twin-engine fighters were used to intercept the bombers as they came and went. These defensive fighters claimed between them the destruction of 23 enemy aircraft, of which the single-engine fighters claimed 19."

For once, Stevens was not numbered among those single-engine fighters. That said, however, post-war analysis shows that the Luftwaffe lost only 11 aircraft, thus representing overclaiming by the RAF fighters to the extent of a little over 50%. Richard was, however, airborne that night and the following interview by author A B Austin, published in the *Daily Herald* on 28 May 1941, was attributed by James Stevens to his late brother:

"It was an old stone farmhouse on the edge of the airfield. Better than most pilot huts. The light was dim. Wouldn't do to go from a bright light into a dark night sky. Take too long to get used to it. We sat by the fire in wicker chairs, and one of the pilots talked very quietly, partly because that was his habit, partly not to disturb his sleeping comrades. 'You know,' he said thoughtfully, 'if you look at it in a detached way, there's beauty in a night Blitz, seen from above. That Saturday night, the 10th of May, when the House of Commons caught it, for instance.'

A typical view of the London Blitz. Author A B Austin interviewed Richard Stevens for the Daily Herald *when Richard described the strange 'beauty', viewed from above, as the flames flickered and danced among the bomb bursts.*

"'I was over London. The heavy bomb bursts were like amber bubbles which seemed to take a surprising time to break and spread. But the incendiaries were the best to watch. They dropped in squares or rectangles. A few points of red and green and yellow light at first, and then the squares would fill in with light like a set piece.'

"Those were the glimpses that floated into his memory like dust motes."

However, Richard was soon back in action and scoring when he made two more claims on the very next night, 11 May 1941. This time, the engagement was much further south, and during what turned out to be one of the last major attacks of the London Blitz. The geographical separation between Hull the night before, and south London this night, is illustrative of the immense 'parish' over which Richard would nightly roam.

In this sortie, he claimed one Heinkel 111 destroyed and another probably destroyed. However, it is difficult with any certainty to establish which aircraft was confirmed destroyed whilst it is assumed that the 'probable' was one of four KG55 aircraft believed to have gone down in the English Channel. Again, the combat report gives us the story. This time, one of the pilots and crew he came up against certainly knew their business as they tried to defend themselves and evade their attacker:

P/O Stevens left Duxford (where he had landed after a previous patrol) at 03.11 hours in a Hurricane I. Landed back at Wittering at 04.27 hours.

He proceeded to north-east London where big fires were raging. AA was seen to the west and P/O Stevens made for this and sighted a He 111 at 03.30 hours at 9,000 feet. AA was bursting near both aircraft as P/O Stevens closed in. He dived and pulled up on port quarter, firing from 150 yards, the aircraft being obscured by red sparks. He then attacked from the starboard quarter below, resulting in a big explosion in the fuselage. The enemy aircraft dived steeply. There was no return fire. A white stream marked its passage into the dense clouds caused by the fires below. P/O Stevens thought it inadvisable to follow so he resumed his patrol and orbited north London, surrounded by AA fire. He dived to avoid the Ack Ack and then sighted a He 111 above and ahead at 7,000 feet at approx. 03.50 hours. As the Hurricane attacked, the enemy aircraft opened fire from the lower gun position. P/O Stevens returned fire at 100 yards and turned sharp to the left giving the top gunner the opportunity to shoot. The Hurricane was hit in one wheel, the main plane and the centre section spar.

Slipping into position and increasing speed, P/O Stevens tried to go below but the enemy aircraft slowed down and he overshot. He remedied this and fired a long burst into the centre section and fuselage as the enemy aircraft came into sight. P/O Stevens stalled and slipped to port whilst the enemy aircraft dived for cloud. P/O

> Stevens got in another burst and registered hits on the centre section and fuselage. The enemy aircraft slid over and appeared out of control. P/O Stevens knew he was hit as the engine sounded rough and so he returned to base.
>
> P/O Stevens believed the enemy aircraft was going down in the Central London area.

For the first time, enemy gunners had scored hits on Richard's Hurricane. A reminder that this was not always a one-sided game. In fact, that very night another Hurricane was shot down with its pilot killed, while a Beaufighter was also hit and damaged by return fire.

In fact, there were no enemy aircraft downed in the area of Central London, and so it could therefore be assumed that the damaged Heinkel slipped away and perhaps managed to cross the coast because there were no Luftwaffe bombers down anywhere on land that night which might be associated with this claim. It would be reasonable to suppose, however, that the damaged aircraft may have been one of those thought to have gone into the English Channel. On the other hand, the earlier claim for a Heinkel 111 destroyed at 03.30 does tie in very neatly to the aircraft downed at Swift's Field, Station Road, Withyham, East Sussex, at almost exactly the same time.

It is known that this aircraft was destroyed by a nightfighter, although no specific claimant has hitherto been attributed to it. In part, this might well be due to claims by more than one other RAF fighter pilot who could have been linked to the Heinkel's destruction. But it would be fair to say that Pilot Officer R P Stevens was a strong contender as the victor. If he was, then it is not too far-fetched to surmise that the Stevens family might well have seen or at least heard the combat from their home on the outskirts of Tunbridge Wells, not more than four or five miles away to the west.

All that remained of another Heinkel 111 strewn across the ground at Withyham, East Sussex, on the morning of 12 May 1941 after possibly being destroyed by Richard Stevens just a few miles from the family home.

Chapter Seven

LONE WOLF

To all intents and purposes, the London Blitz, which had begun on 7 September 1940, came to an end around the time of Richard's claims on 11 May. For now, there was a very noticeable draw-down on nocturnal Luftwaffe activity over Britain. Yet Richard was still on the hunt.

Although the remainder of May passed without further claim, or even any sightings or contacts on night patrols, he continued as before with the now familiar round of routine flying. That routine, though, was broken on 20 May with an important engagement in London when he was summoned to Buckingham Palace to be decorated with his DFC & Bar by His Majesty King George VI. By the time the King had pinned the decorations on his tunic, Richard had confided to his sister, Helen, that he was finally feeling as though he had begun to do some things to earn it. And so he had! For a while, however, he had figuratively to kick his heels at Wittering waiting for the Germans to show, although during nights on which there were no operations – or no German raiders – he could be found in the ops room "seeing what was going on", or else studying black recognition models of Luftwaffe aircraft from every conceivable angle. In rare moments when he was fully 'off-duty', he could be found in the anteroom of the officers' mess reading the works of his idol, T E Lawrence. John Wray, one of the pilots who knew him at Wittering said:

> "It was what was known of Lawrence of Arabia at the time that 'Steve' admired. He regarded Lawrence as 'his own man', determined to do what he thought was right even if it flew in the face of authority. In that, I believe he saw reflected something of himself."

It wasn't until 14 June, though, that Richard saw further action. And, when it came, it was undoubtedly the most dramatic combat in which he had ever been engaged and involved his first use of the cannon-armed Hurricane IIc aircraft, which had been newly delivered to the squadron. It was also an incident where he was exceptionally lucky to escape with his life. Again, the combat report sets out the detail:

P/O Stevens left Wittering at 01.00 hours on a freelance patrol in a Hurricane II (four x cannon)[5]. After flying for 25 minutes, AA fire was observed. He kept to the west of this and 10,000 feet below but turned towards one particularly heavy burst and saw an enemy aircraft flying north at 11,000 feet and 1,000 feet above the Hurricane. Closing to 500 feet below and losing speed he climbed slowly to identify the He 111 by four exhaust flames, cut-out at wing root and its general outline. P/O Stevens fired a one-second burst from 250/300 yards dead astern causing a tremendous explosion in the enemy aircraft which was audible above the noise of the engine. The Hurricane was thrown violently up and turned onto its back. There was no return fire.

Although nearly blinded by the flames enveloping the victim, P/O Stevens could see incendiaries and lumps of burning magnesium falling and fragments of the enemy aircraft striking the ground where explosions continued for 20 minutes afterwards. Whilst north-west of this position, P/O Stevens called Wittering. A fix indicated he was between Royston and Hertford.

Still partially blinded by the explosion he continued the patrol until his vision was back to normal when he could see a stream of oil coming from the leading edge of the port wing. He called the nearest base on Channel C and landed at Debden at 03.03 hours where he found the oil tank to be punctured.

While dramatic, the content of the combat report still has a matter-of-fact ring about the whole episode. In reality, of course, what had occurred was anything but ordinary and was re-told in a rather more colourful fashion by H E Bates in his work *How Sleep the Brave*:

"Often it is possible to get a Heinkel with a one-second burst; but though he was very close he pressed the button a little longer. [sic] The explosion in the Heinkel was immense. It seemed to lift him bodily out of the sky. He seemed to be projected violently upwards and then fall through the vacuum created by the explosion and down on to a table of flame, seeing it gradually

---

5   It will be noted that the combat reports for Richard's night actions were, variously, patrols, interceptions (where he was given W/T guidance towards a target) or freelance patrols. Occasionally, they were 'Fighter Night' ops which are detailed elsewhere. It was clearly the freelance patrols which he favoured, being left to his own devices as to where he went hunting. In this context, he could be 'his own man' as John Wray had described.

break and rise until it grew into walls of fire about him. This fire, after a few seconds, blinded him, so that for a long time afterwards his sight was partially blacked out, his night vision gone. He had only the most confused and painful impression of flying through the flames and out of it and beyond it, upside down.

"It was all very fantastic. He flew on for what seemed a long time, practically blind. When his night vision came back at last, he saw oil spurting and streaming all over the cockpit. He knew that he had to get down. He was a very long way from home and his only hope was a strange aerodrome. He did not know the approaches, but somehow he got down at last, still confused and blinded by that fantastic, inverted projection along a table of flame."

In that one-second burst, Richard's 20-mm cannon shells must have detonated the entire bomb load of what had been a 3./KG28 aircraft (1T + DL, W.Nr 3237) as they slammed into the fuselage. It is in the RAF Air Intelligence A.I.(1g) report, however, that we can find the grim detail of the aftermath:

"Lower Halstow, Isle of Grain, Kent, 02.00 hours 14 June 1941. He 111 H-4. This aircraft was attacked by a nightfighter and blew up in the air, scattering wreckage over an area of 16 square miles. The engines were never found. All that could initially be found of the aircraft and crew were portions of a Leutnant and Gefreiter's uniforms and a portion of a blood-stained map."

The bomber had blown itself to smithereens in a single and most violent detonation. A little closer to his quarry, and Richard would likely have been taken with it. As it was, his fitter, Cyril Mead, had vividly macabre recollections of the engagement's aftermath:

"When we got over to look at the Hurricane the next day, it was a mess. How he landed it in the dark I do not know. The windscreen of the Hurricane had a large hole in it. The oil tank was punctured and dented, and we found blood, hair and bits of bone and human remains stuck to the leading edge of the port wing, whilst the tips of the propeller blades were smeared with blood."

Mead went on to recall that although the damage was repaired, Richard steadfastly refused to let the ground crew clean the grisly remnants from his Hurricane. They remained there as a strange talisman, until the natural effects of wind, rain and general weathering and beating from the airflow gradually removed the sickeningly grim evidence. Roderick Chisholm in *Cover of Darkness* also recounted his memory of the aftermath of this episode:

Pilot Officer W G G Duncan Smith of 603 Squadron was an airborne witness to Richard's dramatic 'kill' on the night of 13/14 June 1941. He is pictured here in Italy, later in the war when he was a squadron leader.

"With some pride [Stevens] pointed to the leading edge of the wing of his Hurricane; it was varnished, but rough, as if sand had been sprinkled on it while it was still sticky, and he explained that what now looked like sand had been found there after that combat, and had been preserved on his instructions as a trophy both gruesome and illuminating."

Of the German crew, and aside from the pitiful clothing remnants which were discovered scattered about on the ground, absolutely no trace of Ltn Hans Arber, Gefr Friedrich Straub or Fw Georg Hochwald was ever found. They have no known grave. However, the mutilated body of the radio operator, Ofw Eugen Geyer, was recovered from the sea off Sheerness Point on 21 June. Having been sitting in the top gondola position, it is likely that he was literally blasted out of the exploding aircraft while his comrades in the centre of the fuselage were simply vaporised; all of them consumed in the intense blast and conflagration caused by the lethal cocktail of high explosive and aviation fuel. Today, Geyer lies buried in the German Military Cemetery at Cannock Chase. There was, however, another airborne witness to the bomber's destruction.

Pilot Officer W G G Duncan Smith of 603 Squadron was airborne in a Spitfire on a hated 'Fighter Night' patrol, operating under the control of Hornchurch, but flying on detachment out of RAF Debden. These nightfighting detachments lasted three or four days at a time, when the pilots were on standby for night ops. Duncan Smith found them especially taxing, with take-offs in the dark quite frightening experiences for a dayfighter pilot. Not only was the Bunsen-blue glare from the exhausts distracting, but he found patrols at night, especially when there was no moon, difficult in the extreme. He described how he flew up and down on patrol lines, his head permanently down in the cockpit and flying on instruments alone. Such was his concentration on just flying the fighter that he found keeping a lookout all but impossible:

"Only once before did I spot a Ju 88, some distance below me, and showing up against the glare of fires along the Thames. I failed to keep my eyes on it for a fraction of a second and lost it as it disappeared into the inky blackness."

But on the night of 14 June 1941, he thought he was going to get lucky.

Guided by Hornchurch control, he saw anti-aircraft shell bursts and headed towards them just as they stopped. Then, in the darkness, he spotted the dark outline of the German bomber. At that moment, streaks of fire and flashes stabbed towards it out of the darkness behind the bomber which immediately took fire. In the glare, he could see a Hurricane – still firing. In moments, the bomber exploded in the very brightest of bright flashes, bits falling in all directions like fiery meteorites. Disappointed to have missed out on a 'kill', he made for Debden but, in a nervous landing, he managed to hit a tree and had to go around again for what was a somewhat dicey descent. He was lucky to get down in one piece. Less lucky was his Spitfire, with a burst tyre, damaged port wing and port flap which, incongruously, now had a tree branch in full leaf growing out of it. All in all, his experiences that night demonstrated the immense difficulty for most pilots of flying and fighting, at night, in a single-seat fighter. In the morning, as he surveyed the sorry state of his Spitfire, he discovered that the victorious pilot was none other than Richard Stevens: "No wonder I had little chance to get the German bomber. I had been queuing up with a real professional."

A week later, on 21 June, Richard was on detachment to RAF Coltishall, Norfolk, where the squadron's aircraft were principally on the lookout for raiders threatening east coast convoys. Having taken off during the very early morning, he saw nothing until 01.50 hours when he spotted a Heinkel 111 near Winterton. He dived to attack and fired a one-second burst which he saw hitting the top of the fuselage. However, it dived away into haze where he lost it. For the German crew, if they did ultimately survive the attack, then they were lucky. The encounters Richard had with German bombers usually only ended one way.

Only two more victims would fall to the guns of the 'Lone Wolf' before the end of that summer while on detachment at RAF Coltishall. The first was on the night of 29/30 June and was again detailed in Pilot Officer Stevens' combat report:

The convoy was travelling north, and P/O Stevens went north and east and then patrolled east of the convoy at 3,000 feet so that the moon was on the other side of the ships. Bombs then exploded and AA fire was seen. P/O Stevens flew once down the convoy about one mile away from it and on the way back he noticed more AA fire. He went through the AA fire and saw an aircraft cross his bows going north-east at 4,000 feet. Turning after it, he kept it silhouetted against the Northern Lights and as the enemy aircraft turned sharp south-east he closed slowly in below and identified it as a Ju 88.

From 300 yards on the starboard quarter he opened fire with a one-second burst and the enemy aircraft continued to go down to the

> south-east at approximately 250 mph. Another short burst resulted in a large flash near the Hurricane. This may have been a cannon shell hitting the discarded hood of the Ju 88 as a large piece of the enemy aircraft shot past the Hurricane on the port side.
>
> A small flame was observed in the enemy aircraft as it went down in a diving turn to hit the sea and when the foam subsided a fire burned on the surface for two minutes. This was seen by Sergeants Fielding and Gudgeon who were patrolling the same convoy in a Defiant.
>
> No return fire. Landed at Wittering at 03.45 hours.

Astonishingly, the report concludes with the note: "Six rounds fired from each of the four cannon."

In other words, just 24 rounds had seen the demise of this Junkers 88. It was not only testimony to the destructive power of 151 Squadron's new 20-mm cannon-armed Hurricanes, but also to Richard's brilliantly unerring marksmanship.

Despite the relative scarcity of 'trade' during the high summer of 1941 for nightfighter pilots like Richard Stevens, another victim came his way again on the night of 6/7 July. Again, he was operating from Coltishall:

The devastating effect of impacts from 20-mm cannon rounds was dramatically illustrated in Richard's combat report of 29/30 June 1941. They are belted here with two rounds of solid armour piercing (the black shell heads) and then two high-explosive rounds.

> P/O Stevens left Coltishall at 23.03 on a night-flying test. Observing flashes to the east he obtained permission to investigate. And whilst proceeding he sighted an aircraft to the north-east crossing his bows at 500 feet. This disappeared before it could be identified but shortly after another one was seen about one mile north-east and just below cloud at 500 feet. P/O Stevens converged carefully, keeping below and identifying a Junkers 88. He dropped back to dead astern and at 300 yards put a one-second burst into the tail. The enemy lower rear gunner fired with his machine gun just before P/O Stevens. The Hurricane was not hit. The Junkers 88 went straight into the sea off Happisburgh. This

makes P/O Stevens with 12 enemy aircraft destroyed at night. Visibility was deteriorating and shortly afterwards he landed at Coltishall at oo.o4 hours.

His victim seems likely to have been a Junkers 88 of Küstenfliegergruppe 606, 7T + HK, W.Nr 5241, which failed to return from operations off the east coast.

Notwithstanding the dramatic victories claimed by Pilot Officer Stevens on 14 June, 30 June and 6 July, the Blitz was over and the numbers of German raiders in the night skies over Britain had diminished exponentially. It meant that for Richard, his targets had all but dried up and apart from the continuation of routine flying for the remainder of the summer there was a real dearth of action. Instead, and between routine flying, he was engaged in giving talks to operational training units and passing on his knowledge and experience of nightfighting which was unsurpassed in the service. It was a role which he hated, and which simply added to his sense of frustration.

Then, with the arrival of autumn, he would claim just two more victories in British skies. Both would end up being surrounded with some drama and not a little inter-unit and inter-service controversy.

It was not until 12 December 1941 that the *London Gazette* published an announcement for the award of the DSO to Richard Stevens, who was by now acting flight lieutenant. However, the citation set out some of the bare detail relating to what was Richard's penultimate victory claim over the British Isles:

"This officer has shown himself to be a fearless and outstanding nightfighter pilot. One night in October 1941, flying at sea level, he intercepted a Junkers 88 off the East Anglian coast. The raider immediately turned and flew towards the continent at maximum speed, but Flight Lieutenant Stevens gave chase and slowly overhauled it. The raider then opened fire with his guns and began to drop his bombs singly. Columns of water were shot up as a result of the explosions, but Flight Lieutenant Stevens swerved round them and, closing in to short range, shot down the enemy aircraft at almost sea level. He has destroyed at least 14 hostile aircraft at night."

As usual, the combat report gives a little more detail:

16 October 1941. Took off from Coltishall at 17.57 hours in a Hurricane IIc (four x cannon) with orders to patrol the outer swept channel. After flying the first leg of the patrol for half an hour at 140 mph he saw an aircraft half a mile away at sea level and going in the same direction. As he closed he saw two smoke trails and the aircraft turned to starboard. P/O Stevens went

A Hurricane IIc of 87 Squadron with its four x 20-mm cannon.

through the gate to catch up and as he did so the other aircraft dropped bombs which exploded under water after an interval just like depth charges.[6] They were followed by five more. P/O Stevens slowly closed on the aircraft and identified it as a Ju 88. Opening fire at 600 yards he saw strikes on the water below. He closed to 400 yards with the enemy aircraft returning fire and weaving violently. P/O Stevens continued to fire when the enemy aircraft was flying straight. He got in a two-second burst when the enemy aircraft was well in the sight ring and he saw the wheels drop. Closing to 350 yards he gave a long steady burst which resulted in a large burst of black smoke and a cloud of spray behind. The enemy aircraft disappeared and when P/O Stevens passed the spot he saw a large circle of disturbed water and no survivors.

Having used all his ammunition, he turned for base. After ten minutes he saw a Ju 88 above and 200 yards in front. P/O Stevens followed, calling for help. After his third call he was answered by another 151 aircraft when P/O Stevens gave course, speed and distance of the enemy aircraft. He also put on his own top identity

---

6   Some German bombs used against shipping were fused in such a way that they would actually detonate under water, rather than on contact with the water. This was a useful device to cause underwater pressure – and damage – to a ship's hulls in the event that they did not score direct hits.

light to guide the other aircraft in the vicinity.

He continued to follow the enemy aircraft until it did a sharp right turn and he saw the convoy ahead. P/O Stevens turned left and flashed DANGER on his downward lights but received no acknowledgement. Bombs were dropped near the leading destroyer and the convoy opened fire.

Landed Wittering at 19.30 hours.

While some detail differs from that given in the *London Gazette* citation, the story is broadly similar, and we now know that the aircraft went into the sea 50 miles off Winterton, Norfolk.

The squadron's operations record book recorded things in a slightly lighter vein: "Pilot Officer Stevens knocks down another. The clumsy devil. Why doesn't he look where he is going?"

After Richard's combat report had been filed a copy was sent to the Royal Navy for the interest of the RN escort of Convoy Plumb. Replying, Lieutenant Commander Mack of HMS *Valorous*, explained that his ship was the flotilla leader and that although no bombs fell near his ship one stick of bombs did fall 100 yards from HMS *Mallard* which was stationed halfway down the convoy on the starboard side. Due to a big gap in the convoy, Mack surmised that Richard had thought it was the head of the convoy and hadn't seen the rest of the convoy. He went on to say that the lights flashed by him may have been of considerable value to *Mallard*, and although no reply was flashed this would have been on account of the fact that it might have attracted the attacker and alerted him as to which ship was a convoy escort. Instead, said Mack, it would be best to communicate with the convoy via the TR.1133 wireless sets with which all coastal convoys had been equipped to communicate with fighter escorts. The only problem was, of course, that Richard was not formally on convoy patrol. As such, his wireless equipment would have been tuned to another channel. It was purely for that reason that he was signalling by lamp.

Nevertheless, his achievements during the 16 October engagement led directly to the promulgation of the DSO award. Typically, it was H E Bates who again provided a colourful backdrop to the events that autumn evening over the North Sea:

"He had seen his family deprived of the earth [sic] and he must have felt that any night when he did not fly was a whole night of wasted opportunity. He went on in this fretful and furious way for the whole summer. 'Oh! Yes, he was quite mad' they'd say. 'Quite mad'. And he had reason to be. They had already decorated him handsomely; now they decorated him again. But what he needed, all that summer, was not decoration but simply the chance to fly, to kill and blow out a few more lights in the darkness across the water.

"The chance did not come until the end of summer. He was out on the sea beyond the Norfolk coast and they say he actually screamed at the sight of a Heinkel. [sic] It was the scream of a man who does not find it possible, even by time and bloodshed, to neutralise a hatred. It was the scream of a whole summer of released fury and boredom and inactivity. He drove the Heinkel [sic] inexorably down to sea level. As it jettisoned its bombs, which threw up huge columns of water, he rose away from those water spouts and then when they cleared he closed again and opened fire. The moment when the Heinkel [sic] struck the sea in clouds of smoke and steam was the moment for which he had waited. It did something to set him free. They decorated him again for that."

How much this event had set Richard 'free' we cannot know, and H E Bates' assertion of the fact could possibly be nothing more than merely artistic licence. However, and although pre-dating the 16 October combat, Richard did write to his sister, Helen, on 27 July and seemed in a far better frame of mind than he was at the time of the letter written to the family earlier in the year. Unfortunately, only two letters written by him ('Dick' to his family) are known to survive. The one to Helen is equally fascinating:

Richard's letter to Helen in which he describes enthusiastically the cannon Hurricane and its awesome munitions.

"Dear Hels,
The big war slackens up. Little wars continue internally. Owl is trying hard. Will do better when I have re-equipped with hi-speed wings!
Have so much to do that a

day of 24 hours is only half long enough.

Have no news that I can give you, but we have a big surprise up our sleeves. Still on Hurricanes, but now have a real rip-snorter. Four 20-mm guns, and more power. It's a killer! A one-second burst and it's all over.

I am about to get wet. Local cocktail party. Fear it will develop into a de-bagging contest. So am preparing.

Will write again as soon as time allows.

All the best,

Dick."

Portrait of Richard Playne Stevens by Cuthbert Orde.

Clearly, Richard had already recognised that the war had slackened off a little, but his second sentence appears to indicate some continuing personal and internal strife. That said, there does seem to be some 'lightening up' in his demeanour through his intention of going to a cocktail party – behaviour not generally associated with Richard by any of those who knew him. As to his remark about the 20-mm cannon being 'killers', and that after a one-second burst it was 'all over', his most recent victory claims were evidence enough of that. Indeed, talking to his brother James of the dramatic effect of the cannon shells, he told him: "I fired at a German flak ship with them once and I was so surprised at the effect that I couldn't help but look round to see if a Royal Navy destroyer was firing at it!"

Cocktail parties aside, the lack of action through the summer was a truly immense frustration. In the words of H E Bates: "He went on in this fretful and furious way for the whole summer." In August, it was with a sense of utterly bored resignation that Richard sat to have his portrait done by Cuthbert Orde. It wasn't an experience he enjoyed, but he had no choice in a matter which was at the Air Ministry's behest.

Moving on again to the month of October, Richard didn't have long to wait after his combat on the 16th before yet another encounter with the enemy lifted his mood. However, the aftermath of the engagement on 22 October didn't exactly cheer him. And although he could not know it, it would be his last battle over British soil, his penultimate victory and his final 'official' one.

When he made out his combat report on that occasion, it was for a 'Junkers 88 destroyed', and while there was no disputing the fact that the bomber *had* been destroyed, it was a case of *who* had destroyed it. Pending the event, claims also emerged from the crew of a Defiant from another squadron and from Anti-Aircraft Command.

With victory claims given such huge kudos, as well as being important for unit morale, ultimately to oil the wheels of promotions and almost provide 'points' towards potential honours and decorations, there was little wonder they were hotly contested if there was ever cause to do so. And in this case, there was.

It was more often than not the case that, on his night patrols, Richard flew directly towards (or into) an anti-aircraft barrage, if there was one. While there was always a risk of being hit, it was a calculated risk which he was prepared to take. After all, he pretty much knew that where there was flak there were bombers. And so it was on the night of 22 October 1941.

P/O Stevens left Wittering in a Hurricane IIc (Z3261) at 20.30 hours on a Turbinlite exercise.[7] During a tight turn he lost contact with the Turbinlite and flew in the direction of considerable AA fire to the north-west. At 21.25 hours he sighted an aircraft at 10,000 feet and flying north-west at 170 mph above him. It was 250 yards away, showing four exhausts, and was not definitely identified but thought to be a He 111.

P/O Stevens closed to 150 yards and the enemy aircraft turned away to starboard and the lower machine-gun position started firing. P/O Stevens gave a short burst, followed by a longer one, as the enemy aircraft continued to turn with the top machine-gun position now firing. Cannon strikes on the enemy aircraft fuselage were seen and it went into steep dive emitting a shower of sparks. It hit the ground and blew up 20 miles south-east of Wrexham.

It has been reported that a Ju 88 was brought down at Adderley at 21.35. Two of the occupants were dead. One baled out and was taken to Market Drayton Police Station.

P/O Stevens landed at Wrexham with ten gallons of fuel left at 22.35 hours and returned to base at 01.35 hours.

As the aircraft descended, Wittering control heard a jubilant pilot calling: "Tally-ho! I've hit him...... Tally-ho! He is going down......Tally-ho! ...He's hit the ground with an awful thump!"

The idea that Richard would be comfortable operating alongside a flying searchlight is, in many ways, laughable. First, he didn't need lights – searchlights, or otherwise.

---

7   Turbinlite was the name given to a Havoc aircraft, fitted with a large searchlight in the nose and flown in conjunction with a nightfighter. When enemy aircraft were spotted, the searchlight would be switched on and the fighter would engage the illuminated target. However, the idea was not deemed a success and ultimately abandoned.

Second, he preferred to work alone and to hunt alone. For that reason, one must cast some doubt on his assertion that he "lost contact with the Turbinlite". For a pilot who could see so well in the dark, and who could spot and follow any aircraft with ease during nocturnal operations, it seems inconceivable that he should have 'lost contact'. Far more likely, given the distant AA fire, is that he became bored with the idea of sticking with the Turbinlite on rigid patrol lines and just slipped away towards a potentially fertile hunting ground – later claiming that he had simply 'lost' the other aircraft in the dark. But the real issue, after the event, was not losing the Turbinlite. It was who was the victor?

On the face of it, Richard's combat report is pretty much conclusive. And again, at face value, none of any others of his surviving combat reports can really be seriously questioned; always reliable, always accurate and always telling it how it was. That, in comparison to many other pilots' reports which are sometimes difficult or impossible to reconcile. So why the debate? Richard fired, hit the target and saw it go down and hit the ground. 'End of', might well be the terminology applied today!

Unknown to him though and at the precise moment he closed on the Junkers 88, a Defiant of 256 Squadron, crewed by a Flight Lieutenant Coleman and Flight Sergeant Smith, was also creeping up on the enemy aircraft. And, by coincidence, it would appear to be the case that both RAF fighters opened fire on the bomber at exactly the same time – the crews of the two fighters being unaware that anyone else was firing. The first intimation that Richard could not claim the German aircraft as destroyed, but only as damaged, came in a teleprinted message from HQ Fighter Command to 12 Group. It read:

> "On 22/10/41 Squadron 256 (Defiants) had a combat in the same area also at 21.30 hours and claim to have shot down e/a in flames. Wreckage of only one aircraft found in vicinity which bears .303 strikes proving that it was shot down by Defiant. Unless wreckage of second aircraft in Market Drayton are discovered, regret cannot admit P/O Stevens claim as higher than damaged at present."

Naturally, Richard and 151 Squadron were most unhappy at this turn of events – the more so when it transpired that Anti-Aircraft Command (2nd Corps) were also putting in a claim. That, however, was robustly dispensed with by both competing fighter squadrons, it being pointed out that the enemy aircraft was flying at 10,000 feet or less and the AA shells were fused at 14,500 feet. Nevertheless, the army initially persisted in its claim, although 12 Group commented on the AA gunners' claim to have fired 24 rounds in three minutes, rather sniffily remarking: "If AA are stating this, then the gun crews were hardly up to the approved standard rate of fire." It was all getting very tetchy. In the end, and although Richard was initially attracted to the vicinity of the Junkers

88 by ack-ack fire, it was ultimately agreed that the bomber was out of the artillery zone and thus not being fired at by the guns. That didn't, however, resolve the question as to who the aerial victor was. However, after some protracted investigations, which included interviewing the surviving prisoners, it was agreed that both fighters had fired simultaneously and were invisible, each to the other. While the prisoners thought they may have been hit by flak, this was explained by the almost point-blank impacts from four Browning .303 machine guns fired up into the belly of the bomber. The German crew could certainly be excused for thinking such a cacophony of heavy impacts to have been a shell burst. However, they maintained that they did not fire back at either of the fighters – the presence of which, in any case, they said they were completely unaware of.

This raised some difficulty with Richard's assertion that he had received return fire, but the apparent anomaly was explained away as having been flashes from the strikes on the fuselage from the Defiant's gunfire, which he had then mistaken as machine-gun fire directed at him. All told, a credible case was made for a shared 'kill', with lengthy reports and arguments presented by both sides which included diagrams explaining how it had all occurred. Honour satisfied, the Defiant crew and Richard were each granted a half share of the claim. It was his first shared victory, and officially his last victory, too. But it was better than just being granted a claim categorised as 'damaged'.

The aircraft had been W.Nr 1376, 7T + CH, of 1./Küstenfligergruppe 606, and it is interesting to review the RAF Air Intelligence 'K' report relating to this episode which is a composite of information gleaned from the two survivors and gives the entire detail of the mission, from take-off up until the point of being shot down:

"Thirty-five aircraft from Schipol were detailed to take part in the attack on Merseyside, six aircraft of 1/606 and five of 2/606 being detailed to attack a grain elevator at Birkenhead.

"The aircraft 7T + CH, which carried two x 500 and two x 250 kilo bombs, took off at 18.57 hours BST, and after crossing the Dutch coast at 400 metres flew direct to the North Sea approximately 53° 30' N and 2° 0' E.[8]

"While flying over the North Sea they climbed through the clouds, which were at 800 metres, during which they experienced icing-up of the leading edges and airscrews. It is said that the new ['Kuton-Nase'] anti-balloon devices reduce the effectiveness of the heating of the leading edges.

"From this point they turned onto a 270° track to make a landfall, flying at 2,500 metres, just south of Spurn Head. They continued to fly westwards and

8   The crew had comprised Ofw Herbert Datzert (pilot), Gefr Karl Hennemann (observer), Uffz Josef Kolar (radio operator) and Fw Erich Neunkirchen (flight engineer).

saw anti-aircraft fire on the north side of the river firing at another aircraft.

"In order to avoid the heavily defended area, the aircraft made a wide de-tour passing south of Sheffield to approach Birkenhead from the south-east. During this period, they saw a heavy searchlight concentration, and what they took to be an anti-aircraft barrage to the north.

"Shortly after turning onto the last leg running up to Birkenhead, and while still well south of Merseyside, they were picked up by a searchlight from behind.

"The pilot successfully took avoiding action by diving 200 metres; shortly afterwards they were picked up by a second searchlight from ahead and the pilot turned northwards towards the target and again evaded the searchlight.

"The visibility was such, that from the height they were flying they real-ised that the target would not be identifiable. At approximately 21.20 hours, when on a north-westerly course, the bombs were released at 100-metre in-tervals. It is probable that they fell on the south bank of the Mersey well short of the target area. The bombs were seen to explode but no further re-sults were observed.

"There was considerable searchlight activity, and although there was a cer-tain amount of anti-aircraft fire it did not appear to be firing at this aircraft and the crew, for this reason, were expecting an attack by nightfighters.

"The two survivors differ regarding the height at which the aircraft was flying at this stage. According to the wireless operator, he had asked the pilot a short time before and was told that they were flying at 3,400 metres having released the bombs from 3,700 metres.

"The observer, who had the opportunity of seeing the instruments for himself, maintains that they were flying at little over 2,000 metres when attacked, having released the bombs from 2,500 metres.

"The pilot had by this time turned for home, and there was a violent ex-plosion immediately underneath the aircraft which illuminated the interior and badly shook the aircraft. The flight engineer was wounded, and the right engine damaged. The revs dropped immediately.

"Some time afterwards – according to one man about 30 seconds, and ac-cording to the other some three to four minutes – a second and similar explo-sion occurred below the nose of the aircraft.

"The observer's left hand and neck were slightly scratched, the wireless op-erator experienced considerable blast and the pilot was almost certainly very severely wounded – he was seen by the survivors crouching in a very tense attitude over the control column.

"The two survivors differ in their opinion as to the cause of the explosion. The wireless operator, who has 92 war flights to his credit, believes that the explosions must have been from medium or heavy anti-aircraft fire.

"The observer, who was on his first war flight, considered that the damage from the second explosion was caused by a 20-mm shell.

"Although the crew were on the lookout for nightfighters, none were seen nor was any tracer.

"The pilot ordered the crew to bale out, and the wireless operator, having jettisoned the roof, left first. The observer followed almost immediately thereafter, but by this time the left wing had already dropped, and the aircraft was starting to spin. While floating down the two survivors heard the aircraft howling to earth, and saw it burst into flames on the ground.

"This aircraft had planned to return to Schipol, crossing the English coast at The Wash and then to skirt round off the Norfolk coast before setting course for Holland.

26 October 1941.
Wing Commander S D Felkin"

The report gives us a fascinating insight into a Luftwaffe bomber crew's story of a raid over Britain and their experience of being shot down, as well as the shock and surprise of being blasted at such close range by both .303 and 20-mm gunfire. The two survivors were lucky. They were also willing to share in some very considerable detail the exact circumstances of the raid, from beginning to end, and going very far beyond the 'name, rank and number' Geneva Convention obligations of prisoners of war.

Notwithstanding the October 1941 victories claimed by Flight Lieutenant Stevens, such successes by RAF Fighter Command – or even Anti-Aircraft Command – were something of a rarity now that the regular procession of raiders over Britain had diminished from a flood to a trickle. Summing it up, the C-in-C of RAF Fighter Command wrote:

"…until the end of the year, the scale of attack was much smaller. Although a few more raids were made on London and the Midlands, the Germans devoted most of their attention for the rest of the year to targets near the coast or at sea, and to minelaying.

"Undoubtedly, the main reason for this change was a new strategic conception by the Germans. Having decided to attack the Russians, they withdrew most of their bombers from the West, leaving behind only a small force to second the German Navy's attempt to blockade the British Isles. To what extent this decision was due to the realisation by the enemy that his night offensive was failing as surely (though not so spectacularly) as his day offensive had failed in the previous autumn, I do not know. But that the 'Blitz' did fail to achieve any strategic purpose is clear enough.

"In eight months of intensive night raiding, the German bomber force did not succeed in breaking the spirit of the British people or preventing the expansion of our means of production and supply. Moreover, the cumulative effect of the ever-increasing losses which the Germans incurred as the defences got under way cannot have been a negligible factor, even though these losses were not sufficient in themselves to have brought the offensive to a standstill.

"To the country as a whole, and everyone in it, the end of the night battle was a great relief; nevertheless, there was a sense in which it came to those under my command, and indeed to myself, as something of a disappointment. An enemy over whom we felt that we were gaining the mastery had slipped out of our grasp. All arms of the defence were working better than they had ever done before; the first five months of 1941 had seen a steady and striking improvement in the results achieved. We were confident – I am confident still – that if the enemy had not chosen that moment to pull out, we should soon have been inflicting such casualties on his night bombers that the continuance of his night offensive on a similar scale would have been impossible."

Clearly, then, Richard was not alone in his sense of disappointment that the night battle over Britain had come to an end. His desire to wage war on the Germans, almost his own 'personal' war, had not diminished and, one night, he was sitting in the Wittering officers' mess with fellow officer George Hamilton. The latter later recalled that night: "I was sitting next to him one evening in the mess when he expressed his opinions of the Germans so violently with a table knife that it finally snapped in two pieces in his hands as he jabbed it into the table."

By this stage, he was the RAF's highest-scoring nightfighter pilot, leading all radar and navigator assisted pilots by a considerable margin – but now he had another job and another posting; this time to 253 Squadron based at RAF Hibaldstow, but with whom he was soon headed south to detachment at RAF Manston. For Richard, the posting was one he would relish. Not only would it involve more night flying, but he would be flying from Britain's airfield which was the closest to enemy territory. And he would be able to go hunting German bombers in more fertile hunting grounds – the Luftwaffe's 'own' airspace over Europe.

Cyril Mead, his fitter, recalled Richard leaving Wittering on or around 12 November 1941:

"He asked me to make and fit a special bracket inside the right-hand side of the cockpit. I asked him what on earth it was for. He replied: 'This!' and thrust a Smith and Wesson service revolver in my hands. I can remember saying to him that it wouldn't really be very much use for shooting down Heinkels or Junkers 88s, and he said: 'No, but it will certainly kill Germans!' I only realised later that he felt he needed to carry a pistol in case he ended up being downed over German-held territory. I'm sure he'd have tried to shoot his way out of things if that had happened! Well, of course, I had no idea at that time what he was about to set out and do. After a few barrel rolls as he departed Wittering, he was off and heading away. It was interesting to me that a pilot being posted out to another squadron took his own 'personal' Hurricane with him. But Stevens did!"

Cyril Mead, and all the others who knew him and had grown fond of and sometimes grudgingly admired him at Wittering, would never see him again.

Chapter Eight

NIGHT INTRUDING

By late summer, the mass German night raids of the Blitz had all but stopped and the frustration felt by Richard at this lack of 'trade' was almost palpable. Having learned his craft, and then honed it to perfection in a little over six months, he was not a man who would have accepted relegation to either training duties or, perhaps, to another nightfighter squadron where his skills as a solitary hunter might not be so well exploited. Already, airborne interception radar was very much coming on-stream with the nascent RAF nightfighter force, and its fitment into what was fast becoming the RAF's foremost nightfighter, the Beaufighter – and very soon the Mosquito – was continuing apace. In these aircraft, the pilots were guided onto the target by a radar operator and only had to use visual sighting during almost the last moments of the chase. None of which would have been to Richard's liking and it would not have suited his modus operandi. First, he would have no longer been the lone hunter. Second, it was the Mk 1 eyeball rather than the Mk 1 radar with which he preferred to hunt. Roderick Chisholm in *Cover of Darkness* summed it up thus: "He scorned Beaufighters and radar."

The fact of the matter was that there were no longer any significant bomber streams to find and to disrupt over Britain where he had once regularly flown, deliberately and perhaps recklessly, into British anti-aircraft barrages. There, he would pick out individual machines with his exceptional night vision, control his Hurricane into the right position and pick off the raiders with his consummate marksmanship. In fact, just flying a Hurricane at night was challenging – let alone finding and engaging the enemy. Often, cockpit canopies would be left open for better visibility. In turn, this allowed the carbon monoxide exhaust effluent to be sucked into the cockpit, making it an inhospitable environment and one where temperatures could also plummet to minus 55°C. The Hurricane, also, could not be left alone to fly itself. This was a distracting factor at night, but with Richard being the master of machine, night sky and quarry, he needed a new role in which to ply his trade. That new 'trade' was succinctly set out in a report by the intelligence officer at RAF Manston in June 1943 into the 'Manston Night Flight' of which Richard had been part. Although compiled some 18 months after the loss of Flight Lieutenant Stevens, the history of intruding operations – and his part in it – is succinctly set out:

"The idea of using the Hurricane as a night intruder probably originated with Squadron Leader Gracie DFC who, as a flight commander with 23 Squadron in April 1941, made a few sorties in a Hurricane I (which was on the squadron's establishment for night-flying training) from Manston to the Lille and Merville areas. He did not have any actual successes, but he saw enemy aircraft on at least one occasion and showed the possibilities of single-engine intrusion (and, incidentally, of using Manston as a base for it).

"The experiment was copied by other squadrons and on 9th May 1941, a Defiant of 264 Squadron using Manston as a forward base, destroyed a Me 110 over Merville.

"When the Germans started their Russian campaign in June 1941, they moved what was left of their bomber force on the Western front to a more discreet distance and ceased to use bases which could be covered by short-range fighters. As a result, Hurricane intrusion lapsed for a while.

"In November 1941, however, the idea received a new and distinguished patron. At that time, Flight Lieutenant R P Stevens DSO DFC and Bar, who had phenomenal success during the past year in destroying enemy aircraft while on freelance patrols over this country, was sent to Manston to break new ground, as 'business' was bad in the Midlands and it was thought that he might be able to tackle the Thames Estuary mine layers, which were paying fairly regular visits in those days – or rather nights.

"The aircraft which Stevens used was a Hurricane IIc which was fitted with long-range tanks and had a maximum endurance, flown economically, of five-and-a-half hours. At that time Manston was being used as a forward base by 23 Squadron, then the only regular intruder squadron, and Stevens very soon saw that here was a form of activity which would pay better dividends than 'stooging' about a night sky which was becoming very sparsely populated with enemy aircraft.

A 23 Squadron Havoc aircraft is prepared for one of the pioneering 'intruder' operations.

"After some discussion he obtained permission to accompany one of the 23 Squadron Havocs on a patrol over one of the Dutch bases, and on 11 December he set off for Gilze-Rijen, formating on a Havoc; the crew of which, incidentally, never saw him from take-off to landing, but his exceptional night vision enabled him to follow them quite easily to the target area.

"The trip was unsuccessful; Stevens remained in the target area for an hour after the Havoc had left, but no aircraft were seen, although there did appear to be some activity. He returned enthusiastic about the possibilities of the operation, however, and it may be said that here was the start of the Manston Night Flight's intruder activities."

Group Captain Tom Gleave, station commander at RAF Manston in December 1941.

When Stevens had arrived at RAF Manston on joining 253 Squadron, the station commander was Group Captain Tom Gleave who had been shot down and badly burned when serving as the CO of that very same squadron during the Battle of Britain. He would later recall:

"Night intruding was in its infancy and 'Steve' was one of the pioneers. He was someone I admired tremendously and although quiet and very much a loner, he was of course imbued with this hatred of the Hun."

Gleave went on to explain that Richard's role at Manston was an unusual one and did not conform to general operating procedures and protocols in the command set-up at either group, squadron or even station level. As such, Gleave recalled, he had a certain autonomy about what he did and how he did it, despite his rank:

"Apart from being a loner, 'Steve' was also granted some kind of dispensation – official or otherwise, I don't know – to fly and fight how he saw fit. I think there was a tacit recognition that he was a bit special. In fact, his night flying and nightfighting capabilities were certainly unique and there was a need to establish the best way to get to grips with the Germans on intruder missions. Not surprisingly, he was regarded as the best man for the job. If not the only man."

Certainly, Stevens was one of the pioneers of intruding – albeit that the tactic had had an embryonic start a little earlier than April 1941 as suggested by the Manston intelligence officer. In fact, in his *London Gazette* despatch, Marshal of the Royal Air Force

Sir Sholto Douglas, wrote:

> "...No. 23 Squadron began to fly 'Intruder' patrols on 21st December, 1940,
> [but] it was not until the early spring that the squadron had many opportu-
> nities of successful action. With better weather and increased enemy activity
> it was then very successful, claiming the destruction of three enemy aircraft
> in March, 1941, two in April, and eleven in May. Thereafter, opportunities
> were again limited. Nevertheless, it was decided that a second 'Intruder'
> squadron should be added to the Command, and No. 418 (RCAF) Squadron,
> equipped with Bostons, began to form in the autumn.
>
> "No. 23 Squadron, originally equipped with Blenheims, re-armed with
> Havocs in March and April, 1941, and received a few Bostons later in the
> year.
>
> "Between 21st December, 1940, and 31st December, 1941, Operation In-
> truder was carried out on 145 nights and 573 sorties were flown, of which
> 505 were by Blenheims, Havocs and Bostons of No. 23 Squadron, and 68
> by Hurricanes and Defiants of Nos. 1, 3, 87, 141, 151, 242, 264, 306 and
> 601 Squadrons, which were employed on this work occasionally on moon-
> lit nights. The destruction of 21 enemy aircraft was claimed, 290 separate
> bombing attacks on airfields were reported, and ten of our aircraft were lost."

Nevertheless, and despite the enthusiasm being exuded, the ratio of RAF losses against
enemy aircraft claimed was not exactly encouraging. While 21 were claimed, the real
total would appear to be nearer to half that. In other words, almost one RAF aircraft
lost for each enemy aircraft destroyed. Worse, with the majority of RAF losses occur-
ring over enemy territory, the pilots or crews were inevitably taken prisoners of war if
they were even lucky enough to survive. And most did not. So, POW or otherwise, they
were a total loss to RAF Fighter Command. On the other hand, any Luftwaffe crews
shot down over German-held territory who were lucky enough to survive an intruder
attack would live to fight another day. On balance, and although it was taking the war
back to the enemy, the sums didn't really stack up. The means simply didn't justify the
end. In fact, it was a broadly similar scenario to that being played out across the same
period in RAF Fighter Command's daytime operations, the 'Circuses' and 'Rhubarbs'
being flown across France and Belgium. Again, the losses were high, and the results
achieved were questionable – and certainly over inflated or exaggerated. Thus, by day
and by night throughout 1941, RAF Fighter Command's lifeblood was gradually being
drained away, and for little worthwhile return. And while the night-time casualties
were more than significantly lower than those by daylight, there was recognition that
a lead needed to be taken in developing RAF intruding tactics. Clearly, there was a per-
ception that there was only one man for the job.

Fighter Pilots' Daring Sea Rescue Off Dungeness

VOLUNTEER fighter pilots, flying in appalling weather a few feet above the sea, brought off a daring rescue of a pilot forced down 20 miles off Dungeness.

They found the pilot, despite thick mist, drizzle and cloud; returned to the English coast and guided rescue launches to the spot.

They were back on their aerodrome within the hour.

It was at 12.50 that a Squadron Leader landed at an airdrome to report that one of his pilots had been forced down in the Channel.

The O.C. of one of the "resident" squadrons asked for volunteers to make a search. He himself was prevented by the doctor from going, as he had baled out himself the previous day and had been rescued from the sea.

There were plenty of volunteers, including a night fighter pilot who was also on the station that day. Five were selected.

They swept the sea less than 100 feet up, circling the area where the missing pilot was said to be. Finally, the night fighter pilot saw the man waving from a dinghy.

While the night fighter pilot circled the spot, two other pilots went to bring a rescue craft. They discovered two launches near the coast and guided them to the spot.

The pilot was brought safely ashore.

Whilst at Manston, Richard participated in a search for an RAF pilot downed in the English Channel and he was the pilot who spotted him and helped to effect his rescue.

Of course, and as we can see from the dates set out in the *London Gazette* piece, the initial introduction of intruder ops had been at a time when Richard was still hunting Luftwaffe bombers over Britain, but just five days after his first intruder flight (the dual operation with the 23 Squadron Havoc) he would fail to return from another intruder sortie over Holland. In the words of Manston's intelligence officer, Stevens had "started something" and, a week or so before his last flight, a Sergeant Scott and Sergeant Gilbert had been detached from 3 Squadron to Manston to study his methods of nightfighting and, with Flight Lieutenant Stevens, to collectively become what was known as the Manston Night Flight.

Now, though, Richard had further recognition of his fighting prowess with the award of the DSO, the citation appearing in the *London Gazette* on 12 December, although notified to Stevens himself some little while prior to this (see page 105). The citation was typically fulsome in its praise.

At some time soon after the notification of his DSO, and consequently shortly before his death, Richard would enjoy a brief family reunion one Sunday during late November (or very early December) when he made the relatively short 'hop' by Hurricane from RAF Manston to the pre-war grass airfield at Penshurst near Tunbridge Wells. His brother, James, recalled the memorable visit and the last time his family saw him:

"My wife and I set off for Penshurst that Sunday from the family home at Frant Road to meet Dick. I think our father came, too. The weather was dull and overcast, but perfectly good enough for flying – especially for someone of his ability. As we waited, he circled the airfield low and then landed and taxied over. One of the ground crew said: 'Watch it boys! This one knows his onions.' Our greeting of him was one of pleasure and pride. Certainly, we were very proud of him and probably made that plain. He, on that score, was very non-committal. No 'side' at all. Anyway, when he got in the car, he took over

Home for the Stevens family during the war was at 14 Frant Road, Tunbridge Wells. It was here that Richard spent some time with his parents and siblings just a few days before he was killed. In this view, one of Richard's cars stands by the front door. During the war, his cars were illicitly powered by RAF aviation spirit!

the driving and somebody suggested we should go to the nearby 'Spotted Dog' pub, and off we set. I can only describe his mood as excitable, and on the way he wound down the window, pulled his service revolver from where he had tucked it in his boot [he would have removed it from his bespoke cockpit bracket and taken it with him for safety when he left his Hurricane at Penshurst. Author], and then fired several times at a notice which said: 'Trespassers Will Be Prosecuted'. Well, he never did like authority and this sign was right by a stile to a public footpath. It was a sign which had annoyed us for years when we were youngsters. Anyway, he fired as we drove past. He didn't even slow down. Probably, he shot from a range of 12 to 8 feet. As I recall, he fired three or four times and each round hit the sign. A bit later, we got behind a silly old so-and-so who was driving in the middle of the road – but Dick's driving 'technique' scared him into pulling over!

"At the 'Spotted Dog', we had a few drinks but then somebody stupidly proposed a toast to Dick's next 'kill'. He didn't like that at all. None of us did, and we left soon afterwards and drove back for an early Christmas lunch at Frant Road. I recall that Dad said he would like to be there when Dick got his DSO, and to go to the party afterwards, and he said: 'Of course, Dad. But there will be some Nautch girls [exotic Indian dancers] there!'

"Back at Penshurst, we all said our farewells. Then, he simply got in his 'Hurribird' and took off into the dusk. There was no goodbye pass. No showy fuss. He just flew off and that was that. On the way home from Penshurst, we were all a bit down. We realised how very close death was to victory.

"And Dick would be dead a few days later."

In all things, planning included, Richard was meticulous. His rigger, AC1 Harold Savage, remembers him being extremely fastidious about his aircraft. He would personally oversee the alignment of his guns and the setting up of the gunsight, and the cockpit's glass windscreen and Perspex had to be absolutely spotless. The walk-around inspections would be done far more carefully than it was by other pilots, and Harold had to accompany him – standing back at a respectful distance as the maestro inspected his aircraft, sometimes twice, and Savage waited for any questions or readied himself to deal with anything needing attention. In the short time he was at Manston, Savage also recalled a row of red swastikas painted under the cockpit rail and a large red question mark painted on the cowling of the aircraft that Stevens regularly flew.

The Spotted Dog pub at Penshurst where Richard celebrated the award of a DSO with family members.

Another fitter, a member of 615 Squadron, was also sometimes detailed to work on his Hurricane at Manston.

Laurie Hale recalled him as being an exacting pilot to work for:

> "Everything had to be done for Stevens without lights. Sometimes he flew with 615. We had to fumble in the inky dark. No lights in the cockpit were to be switched on, as he didn't even want the dull luminous glow from the fluorescent instrument dials. We couldn't even use shielded torches. The blackout was never as dark until 'Steve' Stevens was around! He would spend an hour in the flight hut in complete darkness before taking off, but he had a line of dim blue lamps to guide him from dispersal as a taxiway which ran across a road to the runway. On one night the road was his undoing. In his impatience to get going, he taxied too fast across the road and smashed off his tailwheel on the edge of the tarmac."

As Laurie Hale indicated, it was certainly the case that Richard Stevens also sometimes flew with 615 Squadron from Manston, albeit that he was on the strength of 253. This is borne out by an entry in the RAF Manston operations record book on 15 November 1941, just three days after his arrival on the station:

> "Flight Lieutenant Stevens (attached 615 Squadron) in Hurricane took off 19.17 hours. Over Eastchurch aerodrome followed ack-ack burst which left traces of burning material for three to four seconds. As pilot closed in a dark

object leaving a trail of silvery particles fell rapidly earthwards. Patrol continued and finished without event. Dark night. Moderately clear. No moon."

Once, when flying from Manston, Richard went into a towering rage after landing from a patrol. Aircraftsman and MT Pool driver, Grant Taylor, was often detailed to drive Flight Lieutenant Stevens from the mess at Westgate-on-Sea to RAF Manston and the dispersal point. Once there, he would wait in the cold dispersal hut for his return from flying, but one particular occasion stood out in Taylor's memory:

"He landed after a patrol, furious that the anti-aircraft guns had stopped firing at enemy aircraft because a friendly aircraft – his Hurricane – was in the area. He grabbed a phone in the hut and let rip about the guns having stopped firing, saying that it was helping to guide him to the enemy. He was livid. But the thing I remember mostly was that he was in such a rage when he came in the hut that he threw his service revolver down on the table where I was sitting. He threw it down with such force that it spun round and round and round on the chamber. It was a bit like a rather strange version of Russian roulette, and each time the barrel pointed my way I literally flinched. Well, it lightened things up a bit. It made him smile!"

In many ways, the Manston era saw the golden age of intruding and was conducted during a period when the Luftwaffe was seemingly oblivious to the risks now being posed by RAF nightfighter aircraft flying over the enemy's European bases. So secure did the Luftwaffe feel from the risk of intervention that their airfields had elaborate lighting systems, its aircraft also flying with wingtip navigation lamps lit up and their landing lights on. Such was the almost garish extent of the illuminations that it quickly became apparent that all the RAF intruder aircraft needed to do was to lurk around the circuits of these lambent German airfields and wait. There was irony, however, in the fact that some of the German aircraft returning to their home bases were themselves 'intruders' who had been on sorties lurking over the somewhat darker airfields of East Anglia waiting to catch RAF bombers returning from 'ops' over Europe. Now, the tables were turned.

The hunters had become the hunted, because it was from Gilze-Rijen that another nightfighter unit, NJG 2, were operating their night intruder missions over Britain, stalking returning RAF bombers and shooting them down as they returned home. All things considered, the Luftwaffe ought to have been more cautious and better prepared for such eventualities arising over their own airfields. Again, H E Bates summed it up: "They are the intruders who look for Christmas trees: the 'dromes with their landing lights burning and the red and green and yellow eyes of returning planes."

Surprisingly, and notwithstanding the fact that intruder operations had already begun to reap particular successes from early 1942, it took until July of that year before the Luftwaffe had finally cottoned on and changed its night landing and airfield lighting procedures. Until that time, RAF pilots were often able to intercept aircraft as they flew down the Lorenz landing beams towards their brightly lit airfields. A number were not actually shot down, either, but simply collided as they loitered in holding areas if danger was perceived near their home airfields. Yet more of them simply flew into the ground whilst taking avoiding action at low level, while others crashed when trying to make rapid landings after being panicked in their attempts to evade an intruder. All told, Flight Lieutenant Stevens had certainly 'started something'! Sadly, however, his foray into the world of intruding would be all too brief.

We thus return to 15 December 1941, and to his rigger at RAF Manston, AC1 Harold Savage, for his recollection of that particular night:

> "It was a bitterly cold night and there were clouds in the sky. He came out by himself and walked to the all-black Hurricane. It had long-range tanks, no squadron markings or letters and just the usual RAF roundels and fin markings.[9] I strapped him in and wished him 'Good luck!' He immediately taxied out and took off without delay. Very soon, the red and green navigation lights flicked off as he passed beyond the snow clouds and away from our sight as we lost track of him in the eastern sky."

Also flying from Manston, but using it as a forward operating base, were 23 Squadron and their Havoc aircraft. Normally based at RAF Ford, the squadron would send over two or three aircraft from each flight for two nights at a time, and then rotate with other aircraft when they returned to Ford. One of their pilots was Pilot Officer W A 'Dickie' Bird DFC, who had a clear recall of Richard as well as events surrounding the night of his loss:

> "It was at Manston that I met Stevens and we used to get talking in the mess before going down to the airfield for readiness. In fact, I also recall that he distinguished himself in my life by buying me my very first half pint of an extremely tasty Kentish brew! Over the beer, I recall saying to him that it was extremely 'dicey' going over the other side on just one engine. He replied, laughing, and said: 'Well, when one of your engines stops the other one just

---

9   It is interesting to note that Cyril Mead's memory of Richard taking 'his' Hurricane with him was accurate, in that Hurricane IIc, Z3465, is shown on the aircraft record card (AM Form 78) as being delivered to 151 Squadron on 1 June 1941 and then being allocated to 253 Squadron on 20 November 1941, roughly corresponding to the date of his posting to that same squadron.

drags you into the ground! So, what's the difference?!'

"He would take off from Manston at night, an undulating grass airfield, without a flare path if he was in a hurry and then climb to the very apex of the searchlights and flak over Dover and search for his prey. Occasionally, he would fly over the other side in the company of one of our aircraft and later he would come back on his own.

"On the night of his last trip he rang me at dispersal to see if we were taking off soon. I told him that all was quiet, and we were remaining at readiness. So, he said he would go off on his own and asked me for the course to steer to Gilze-Rijen. He said he was going to shoot up the airfield or any aircraft that were around. I gave him the course, and details of the route in, but I warned him that from personal experience the defences there were extremely intense, especially if they had aircraft operating.

"We were not ordered off that night and sadly he did not return. I often wondered what happened to him."

Richard departed from Manston in Hurricane IIc, Z3465, heading enthusiastically and confidently out over the North Sea and towards his new-found hunting ground over the Netherlands. In the usual inimitably dull style of operations record books, the squadron's orderly office clerk was assigned to write up the detail: "19.40 hours. Flight Lieutenant Stevens left Manston to go to Gilze-Rijen airfield in Holland via Overflakke."

By its very nature, intruding was arguably an even more solitary affair than was nightfighting over Britain, and with wireless traffic minimal to non-existent. It also involved long and risky flights over the sea, before arriving over hostile enemy-held territory. Thus, when Stevens took off that night and headed into the inky blackness over the North Sea he was, more than ever, the 'Lone Wolf'. Exactly what happened on his last flight is unknown and we can only assemble the facts as we know them and draw our conclusions from that.

Earlier that evening, 24 Junkers 88s of III./KG30 had taken off from their base at Glize-Rijen for operational flights but now, as Richard arrived in his Hurricane to loiter overhead, the Ju 88s began to straggle back home. With them, were another two Junkers 88s: nightfighters of NJG 2. Unconcerned by any risk that might arise from enemy aircraft, the bombers had their wingtip navigation lights and their landing lights switched on, and, of course, the airfield itself was also very well lit. In fact, and to illustrate just how brightly Gilze-Rijen actually was illuminated, Peter Stahl, a Ju 88 pilot with 6./KG30, talked about it in his book *Diving Eagle*: "On the way out, we fly once more past the whole red-white-green light display of Gilze-Rijen before leaving it for the darkness in the west."

There can be no doubting, then, just how much of a beacon Gilze-Rijen (and other Luftwaffe airfields) must have been to RAF night intruders. Although flying from a different airfield, another Luftwaffe pilot, Leutnant Klaus Conrad of Stab III./KG26 described it thus:

> "Our airfield illuminations at this time were like brightly lit funfairs, and it wasn't surprising they began to attract RAF fighters when the British got a bit more adventurous. A bit like moths to a candle flame. I was taken POW in Britain during April 1941, but I later found out that some of my best friends died because of this stupidity; almost home from a sortie, then killed minutes from safety."

Leutnant Klaus Conrad.

In fact, it almost didn't require the marauding RAF pilots to have the exceptional night vision of unusual men like Richard. All they had to do was to sit above the enemy airfields. And wait. Richard had done just that, and although we cannot know the exact circumstances of his demise on that fateful night, the possibility cannot be excluded that his night vision had been impaired by the comparatively bright glare out of an otherwise inky darkness.

What we do know is that Richard, having selected the first returning bomber that he saw, dived down in the attack just as the Junkers 88 was on its final approach, the pilot concentrating on setting the aircraft up for landing. No doubt the crew were relaxed and off their defensive guard. After all, they were 'home', now. The pilot, meanwhile, would have been focused on nothing else but the landing. In every respect, the bomber was a sitting duck.

In his attack (timed by the Germans as 21.38 hours) it was inevitable that Richard would succeed. And indeed, he did. Just short of the runway threshold, dozens of 20-mm cannon shells slammed violently into the unsuspecting bomber at almost point-blank range and immediately set it ablaze. For the startled crew, it was perhaps fortunate that they were almost on the ground. Hurriedly, and just as the Hurricane roared past them and veered away, the shaken bomber pilot managed to get the burning Junkers 88 down in more-or-less one piece. They had no idea what had hit them, and it had all been so sudden. Certainly, the German airmen were lucky to escape with their lives, and although the bomber was recorded as '95% damaged' (i.e. a write-off) only one of the crew was injured, suffering just a broken collar bone in the mad scramble to exit the aircraft, shown in Luftwaffe records as 4D + FR, W.Nr 1186. It was quite likely, however, that Richard was banking around to come back on a strafing run on the burning bomber – just to finish the job, and exactly in what was his trademark style – when something went horribly wrong. Whatever it was, it was catastrophic.

Although attention by personnel on the ground at Gilze-Rijen was now focused on the unfolding drama of the blazing Junkers 88, they briefly heard the throaty roar of the Rolls-Royce Merlin of the Hurricane as it roared away, banking around low in the night sky as it passed over the end of the south-west-north-east runway. Then, attentive lest the marauding fighter should return, they noticed that its noise quite suddenly stopped. Its cessation ending with a loud thump. The Hurricane had hit the ground violently about 600 yards from the runway's end, coming to rest in a meadow on the outskirts of the little settlement of Haansberg. When would-be rescuers reached the scene, they found the all-black Hurricane in a crumpled heap with its engine partly embedded in the soft soil. It was still recognisable as a Hurricane, just, albeit that it had hit fast and hard, having seemingly been flown into the ground. Slumped in the badly crumpled cockpit was the lifeless body of its pilot, Flight Lieutenant Richard Playne Stevens, DSO, DFC & Bar.

In the space of little under a year, he had achieved more as a fighter pilot than the majority of others ever achieved in an operational career spanning the entire duration of the war. As he completed the flying logbook of the now absent pilot, an RAF clerk dispassionately entered: "Flying Hours for 1941: 323".

What had caused the Hurricane to crash remains unclear to this day and we can only speculate. What we do know, however, is that no fire was reported as having been directed towards the Hurricane, either from ground defences or from the

The shattered wreckage of Richard's Hurricane at Haansberg, just outside Glize-Rijen airfield, after its loss on the night of 15/16 December 1941.

Junkers 88. It had all been far too sudden and so completely unexpected for that. We also know that Richard had followed the Junkers 88 down, almost to the runway, and must therefore have been flying at extremely low altitude as he roared away and prepared to swing around for either a strafing run on the burning Junkers 88 or to re-join the circuit and hunt for other victims. Low enough, certainly, for there to be no margin for error in piloting skills when flying so close to the terrain. If we can rule out hostile fire as the reason for the crash, we are left with only two options; failure of engine or airframe or pilot error. On balance, the former two are probably the least likely. Which leaves us with the most likely: pilot error.

If the cause of the crash was a mistake on the part of the pilot, we have to remember that pilots of the period were often flying at the extremes of physical and mental endurance, and sometimes in conditions of considerable stress and frequently in absence of light or in bad weather where, ordinarily, flying would have been deemed too risky. Additionally, and interestingly, his CO on 151 Squadron, Squadron Leader J S Adams later said of him:

> "He was not a good pilot. His flight commander described him as ham fisted because he broke several Hurricanes when he joined the squadron. But he was a clever pilot. His peacetime experiences had made him a shrewd bad weather flier and he could always get his Hurricane back to Wittering under the most atrocious weather conditions."

Men like Richard were, though, inherently risk takers who often took chances. He certainly was such a pilot, and notwithstanding his bad weather skill, his hawk eye marksmanship and his night vision capability, there are other human factors which must be taken into consideration. First, his age. Certainly, he was very much older than most fighter pilots of the period and although not in any way an 'old' man, it is a fact that pilots of such an age had reactions that were already slowing up quite significantly when compared to their teenage or early twenties counterparts. And at such a low altitude, it only needed a nanosecond to make all the difference between life and death. Secondly, we need to consider that although he was a 'steady' pilot with exceptional night vision, he was not regarded at all as anything of a careful pilot. In fact, and on top of Squadron Leader Adams' later assessment, he had initially been noted as 'too excitable to fly' when he first joined the RAF. And even if one might question his supposed sheer hatred of the enemy, and a desire to destroy them wherever and whenever he could, one cannot doubt that care for his personal safety had diminished with the death of Frances. Maybe these factors all came into play on that fateful night. What is certain, however, is that his last victory at Glize-Rijen was different to all the rest.

The majority of all of his victories had been gained at considerable altitude, of course, and many of them resulted in his own aircraft being thrown about the sky from slipstream effects, explosions or merely through his input to the controls to avoid defensive fire, the enemy changing course, exploding debris etc. In all those instances, Stevens had the comfort of several thousand feet of sky beneath him to sort things out. Over Gilze-Rijen, there was no such comfort zone, no empty space left beneath him in which to manoeuvre or re-position. Turning, fast and so very low over a terrain which was all but invisible, was a manoeuvre which held all manner of risks – including the danger of spinning into the ground or flying into unseen buildings, trees and electricity cables, for example. And if the aircraft had entered a spin, it would have been non-recoverable from this altitude. And then, of course, there was the light.

Could it also have been that the sensitively attuned night vision of Richard Stevens had been impaired? Impaired by the 'light show' that had been Gilze-Rijen airfield, and then by the glare of the blazing bomber? Again, we know from his other combats that fire, explosions and bright flashes nearly always resulted in some disturbance to his night vision. In that respect the physiological reactions to light in Richard's otherwise remarkable eyes, especially during conditions of darkness, were no different to anyone else's. And if that were the case over Gilze-Rijen, and when flying so close to the ground, then it is likely to have been a contributory factor if not *the* actual cause. Even the best pilots make mistakes. And under these exacting circumstances there was simply no margin for error.

Back at Manston, and as the operational duration of the Hurricane came and went, it gradually dawned on everyone that Richard Stevens was not coming home. A sense of gloom descended over the airfield where, during recent days, there had been a sense of buoyed-up anticipation and optimism that the RAF's highest-scoring 'Cats Eyes' night-fighter pilot was about to embark on a new facet of his career, and to lead taking the fight back to the Germans over their own airfields. Tom Gleave later recalled:

> "I was in the officers' mess, waiting. Then, the ops room rang through to say they had heard 'Steve' calling, but they could not make out what he was saying. Then, nothing more was heard from him. As the night ticked away, the sad truth dawned on us all."

It was left to the intelligence officer at Manston, Flight Lieutenant H J Smith, finally to send the official signal that their pilot was overdue:

> "The Hurricane with auxiliary wing tanks had an endurance of about three and a half hours, so unless he had used a lot of boost or had navigational or headwind problems, he should have had ample time to return to Manston. I remember waiting until about 23.30 hours before sending a signal to HQ 11 Group reporting his take-off on intruder operations against enemy aerodromes and adding the words: 'He has not returned and is now beyond maximum endurance.'"

As a result, the orderly office clerk was detailed to add a rider to the earlier text in the entry regarding the departure to Gilze-Rijen. It read: "[Flight Lieutenant Stevens]...has failed to return to Manston."

The bright star that had been the 'Lone Wolf' had been snuffed out before this exceptional pilot had even had a chance properly to hone the skills necessary to perfect flying and fighting as an intruder. Had he done so, and had he had the time and opportunity to grapple with and to grasp the new challenges and skill sets required for intruding, then there is every reason to suppose that he would have become a leading exponent of that 'art', too. Fate, though, decreed otherwise.

At Glize-Rijen, as crews battled to extinguish the burning Junkers 88 sitting on the runway, a degree of panic had set in on the airfield which resulted in the rapid extinguishing of the bright airfield lighting. Meanwhile, other aircraft in the circuit or on approach to land were

> Officers' Mess,
> Royal Air Force,
> Doone House,
> Westgate-on-Sea,
> KENT.
>
> 17th March, 1942.
>
> Dear *Mr Stevens*,
>
> Thank you very much indeed for the two drawings of "Steve". I shall prize mine very much, and I know the Mess will be very pleased indeed to have the one of him sitting in the cockpit of his aircraft.
>
> I am enclosing your book, autographed as you requested, which I am very glad indeed to do for you.
>
> Hoping to have the pleasure of meeting you one day soon.
>
> Yours *sincerely*
>
> *Tom Gleave,*
>
> S.A. Stevens, Esq.,
> 14 Frant Road,
> Tunbridge Wells,
> KENT.

A letter from Tom Gleave thanking Richard's father for a print of the Eric Kennington painting of Richard in the cockpit of his Hurricane which was hung in the officers' mess.

told to hold by flying control. For at least one other Junkers 88, 4D + HT, the landing delay was critical. In fact, with tanks already depleted from a long-range operational flight, the bomber simply ran out of fuel and crashed, although further details are not known. Although the particulars of that final combat could not be known back in Britain, Flight Lieutenant R P Stevens can now assuredly be granted one extra 'kill' to his official score. It was quite likely as well that he contributed indirectly to the loss of the other Junkers 88 which ran out of fuel.

When his body was removed from the wreckage by the Germans, Richard was initially buried in Zuylen Cemetery, Breda. Post-war, however, he was re-buried by the Imperial War Graves Commission (now Commonwealth War Graves Commission) at Bergen op Zoom Military Cemetery where scattered British and Commonwealth casualties from various parts of the Netherlands were concentrated. Today, he lies there in Plot 23, Row B, Grave 4.

Eventually, and via the usual Red Cross information routes, his death was confirmed to the British authorities and notified to Richard Stevens' parents on 14 January in a

Top: Richard's original wartime grave marker.
Bottom: His grave today in the CWGC Ceme-
tery at Bergen op Zoom.

telegram which read:

"Mr and Mrs S A Stevens, Everseley, 14 Frant Road, Tunbridge Wells, Kent.

7.30

(Noted as received 8.19 pm)

From Air Ministry Kingsway P4.

Deeply regret to inform you that according to information now received from the International Red Cross Society your son 87639 Acting Flight Lieutenant Richard Playne Stevens DFC is believed to have lost his life as the result of air operations on December 15th. His wife has been informed. The Air Council express their profound sympathy. Under Secretary of State."

Since Mabel was still his wife, and thus next-of-kin, it is assumed that a telegram was similarly sent to her where she was then residing, which was with a family member at Laine End, Ditchling, in East Sussex.

Back at Manston, on 13 January 1942, the orderly office clerk had another entry to make: "A signal from Air Ministry, Kingsway, (P4) states that a telegram from the International Red Cross Society, quoting Berlin information, states that Flight Lieutenant Stevens is dead."

It was not until a little later in January 1942 that Richard Stevens' death was finally announced in the British press, although the details of some of those announcements have since been taken as gospel by those who have later sought to write or comment on his RAF career. One such report, which has been quoted or used more than once in post-war commentary, ran under a headline reading: 'Nightfighter Ace Dies on Day Sweep'.

The copy then went on to say: "Flight Lieutenant Stevens died not during a night flight but on daylight operations last month. He failed to return in his Spitfire from a sweep over the islands off the Dutch coast."

Upon such misinformation are historical facts born. And in the case of Flight Lieutenant R P Stevens, such 'facts' are legion. Of course, it is possible that the published information was intentional; designed to feed falsehoods to the Germans and throw them off the scent about intruding operations. Such falsehoods, though, have certainly thrown plenty of others off the scent in the intervening years. But, on the other hand, why try to mislead the Germans about the nature of his demise when they had found his body and knew full well the circumstances? However, at the time these news reports were put out, the Red Cross notification of his death had not yet come through and the Air Ministry may have guessed, wrongly, that Richard Stevens had met his end in the North Sea. As such, they would likely have wished

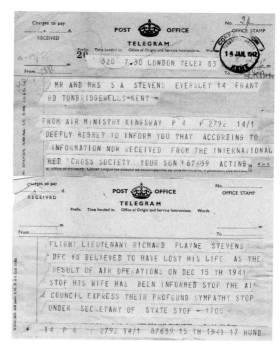

The fateful telegram of 14 January 1942, informing the family that Richard's death had been confirmed. Up until that point he was simply 'missing in action'.

to hide the true nature of his intruder mission from the enemy.

Rather more measured and factual, however, was a broadcast on the BBC Home Service by Group Captain William Helmore of the Air Ministry, who regularly spoke to the nation of the RAF's prowess in the air via wireless. His broadcast at 9.25 p.m. on Thursday, 5 February 1942, should surely stand as the ultimate epitaph for Richard Playne Stevens. Here is a transcript of the broadcast:

> "The other day, from half a column of newspaper, I learned that 'Cat's Eyes' Stevens – that prince among nightfighters – had gone down in offensive patrol over enemy territory.
>
> "I felt on reading this as if a little light, that had flickered for a while against the background of war, had suddenly gone out and left no trace.
>
> "I knew 'Cat's Eyes' Stevens – I have one of his reports in my drawer describing a gallant night experiment with the cold accuracy of a railway timetable, and I want to give him and all he represents such obituary as I can.
>
> "I last saw him a few days ago in Eric Kennington's masterpiece which

hangs in the National Gallery. The face is floodlit by the instrument panel lights for the artist has captured something of the eerie atmosphere of night flying – the feeling of tenseness just before take-off – the curious elongated smoky-green eyes beneath upward-arching brows, which gave 'Cat's Eyes' his nickname, looking forward in a strange, unfocussed way as if into infinity.

"Three times on separate nights those eyes sought out and followed to destruction two enemy night raiders, and once in a screaming dive from twenty-five-thousand feet he swooped down nearly to the ground – bursting an ear drum in the process – to get an enemy whose faint shadow that mysterious sight had somehow sensed against the dim background of the earth five miles below.

"The light which was McCudden, Ball, Mannock – and their successors in the air chivalry of this war – will never go out. The loss of such men is something more absolute even than the loss of a battle, for a battle may be re-fought, but the great fighters of the air are re-born only a few times in a generation. They are re-born because they have something to pass on to flying posterity – not just a little light – but a torch which even the humblest pupil sees on his first solo, and sees again as he runs his sights over his first Hun, and sees yet again, brighter every time, as his score mounts upwards towards the level of these immortals.

"Let us salute – not only a brave man in passing – but an ideal of service which might have been handed down from the Twelve Legions of Angels. Goodnight."

In his assessment that upon Richard Stevens' death "...a little light had gone out and left no trace" there was a remarkable degree of prescience on the part of Group Captain Helmore. For it was certainly the case that during his short career as a nightfighter pilot, really spanning just one remarkable year of achievement, Richard's fame had grown in the eyes of the British public. But, when he died, his fame all but died with him. There were still four long years of war for other heroes to come and to go. Those who became famous and retained their fame were, very often, those who were lucky enough to survive and to tell their tale. Of these, it became fighter pilots like Bader, Lacey, Duke, Stanford-Tuck, Johnson – and Cunningham in the nightfighter role – who were, and still are, well known in the eyes of the British public. All of them, of course, survived. And all of them either wrote autobiographies or had biographies written about them. Of these tomes, most were 'of their time'. A genre apart. And ripping yarns, at that. Imagine, had Richard survived, how much of a 'ripping yarn' his would have been! Speak to those who will know of Bader and his ilk, and tell them of R P Stevens, and the response will often be: "Who?"

On the other hand, and if he has been almost overlooked in Britain, Richard Stevens is not entirely forgotten in the Netherlands. His exploits, and his death, have often been written about – including in *Vijf Jaar Luchtfront* by van den Hout, Klerks and van Riel, 1986. Other times, too, he has been remembered in the media there. Touchingly, in 1990, an unknown Dutch woman wrote of him:

"It is All Souls' Day in Holland and although his name and fame is not remembered by English men and women, it is remembered by me – a Dutch survivor of the German occupation. Today was a beautiful autumn day, and above the sun was shining and the trees were changing colour. On the grass were many leaves from the chestnut trees, making a beautiful blanket over the grave of Richard Playne Stevens DSO, DFC & Bar, as we bent down and gently placed flowers against his headstone."

Chapter Nine

ERIC KENNINGTON

Eric Kennington.

In his book of RAF pilot and aircrew portraits, *Drawing the RAF* (Oxford University Press, 1942), there appears a colour plate of Kennington's famous painting 'Readiness' depicting a pilot representing Richard sat in the cockpit of his Hurricane prior to night ops. Further on in the same volume there is a reproduction of his painting 'Stevens' Rocket', thus marking him out as the only subject in the book who is represented twice. Perhaps this double recognition is a subtle pointer to the special bond which existed 'twixt Kennington and Richard, and which certainly went beyond anything that was just an artist and sitter relationship.

The nature of the closeness between the pair was set out in an undated letter sent by Eric Kennington to Richard's father at some time shortly after his son's death. Scribbled in pencil on the lined pages torn roughly from a notebook, it is a letter which is both enigmatic and ambiguous in almost equal measure:

"Dear Stevens

I fear that I must move about and cannot lunch with you, but I have a patch of spare time now to write.

When I went to Wittering, Stevens almost ran across the room greeting me without hesitation. He had read the *Seven Pillars* well and connected me with TEL. We started a quick intimacy because we were both 'odd' and sympathetic. There are so many 'odd' men in my profession that I was very much at home with him and knew immediately that along with his 'oddness' there were high gifts and intelligence approaching genius. This was not recognised by the others. Not even by the very odd OC. Surely there was a difficult relation between those two as there might easily have been under another OC. Genius is sometimes a nuisance in the services, and Stevens I believe had some of the characteristics of a child. He saw much further than his fellows, and so clearly, but could not realise they were honest in what appeared comparative blindness. He easily opposed them and was quickly put out and so they did not follow his leadership – for he was by nature a leader. Though he had not arrived at the condition of establishing himself as such and having a team obey him smoothly.

To be 'Lone Wolf' was deep in his nature, and you can imagine what a harmony existed between him and myself. I soon lent him *The Mint* by TEL and enclosed is his letter left in its pages.[10] I think that book by another 'Lone Wolf' revealed to him the patterns of his own separate existence, made him understand all about a person whose spirit is solitary and so helped in the adjustment to the community which is so necessary to the odd ones.

He probably learned a bit from me because of my extra twenty years, for at his age I was I think extremely similar. He, to me, was just 'the artist', and my power is what you know. His was manifesting itself for the moment in supernaturally sensing the 'planes in the dark and then acting normally but with superb courage and decision and skill. He wished to go up every night that there were raiders over Britain, but of course other responsible folk did not believe that he could see to land in the fog and rain etc. This caused a sense of frustration and reminded me so much of myself, John, Epstein etc. He was exactly the same in nature.

I was personally fond of him for he seemed to me lovable. We planned things, visits to my parents etc. He never once mentioned his wife and son. He inspired me to do the picture 'Stevens' Rocket' because his description was so vivid that I could draw the picture. He made a rough drawing of the incident for me. The picture was made up of the portrait I drew of him, and notes made while he sat in his 'plane waiting for orders. I never meant this to be a portrait, deliberately altering the lower portion of his face so that the picture would do for all pilots. This put him out. He expected a true portrait of himself. I went with him to examine the remains of one of his victims. Everything he did interested me. He went to leave, and his lightning brain selected only what would teach him – new devices and parts of machines, gadgets etc. and completely ignoring the smoking German air gunner. When interviewing the live prisoners in Kettering jail he was so respectful, considerate and without hostility that the German stood and talked to him without any embarrassment and answered his questions simply. Of course, he was entirely without malice towards the enemy, as the best fighters are, but with

---

10   The letter referred to, on RAF Wittering notepaper, simply stated: 'Dear Mr Kennington, How much this has meant to me I can never express. Thank you. R P Stevens.'

The handwritten letter sent by Kennington to Richard's father.

a most sustained intention of using all his unusual power to defeat them. In that again he was an 'artist'.

While I first knew him, he was not contented, bothered by several things. Later he became more serene, and Doc Walker, his very good friend, wrote how tranquil he became a short time later.

Many of my friends have gone but Stevens' loss meant an unusual blank. Please forgive me for only this scribble. Life presses on one and time is too occupied. I am just off to my home for a short visit. All my best wishes to you.

Sincerely

Eric Kennington.

PS I shall feel the presence of Stevens all my life."

Kennington, an official war artist in both world wars, had seen in 1938 that another war was inevitable, and he therefore approached the Home Office with proposals to set up a group who would work to design camouflage schemes for large public buildings. No doubt prompted by events during the Spanish Civil War, and the likelihood that towns and cities would become targets during air raids, a central Air Raid Precautions unit had already been set up and it was here that Kennington worked with others until the outbreak of war itself. Then, and turning his attentions in a rather more artistic direction, he began to produce pastels of Royal Navy officers for the War Artists' Advisory Committee. However, he became frustrated by the WAAC's inaction in engaging him formally and resigned from that organisation to command a small Home Guard unit at Ipsden. Then, as the war gathered pace, the WAAC wanted him back and offered him a full-time commission to work under contract for the Air Ministry. It was a role that Kennington would cherish, and one which would bring him into contact with Richard Stevens when he found himself posted to RAF Wittering in March 1941.

In his letter, Kennington speaks of Richard 'almost running across the room' to greet him on his arrival at Wittering and from this we see there to be no doubting of his absolute joy at Kennington's posting. The reason was simple; he was almost fixated on the works of T E Lawrence and it was Kennington who had illustrated and been appointed art editor for *Seven Pillars of Wisdom*. Indeed, Kennington had become a very close friend of Lawrence and spent the first half of 1921 travelling through Egypt, Jordan, Syria, Lebanon and Palestine with him and drawing portraits of Arab subjects. Such was his closeness to Lawrence that in 1935, Kennington was to serve as one of the six pallbearers at his funeral. He would later create notable busts and sculptures of Lawrence of Arabia, including a bronze in St Paul's Cathedral and the stunning effigy of him in Wareham Parish Church, Dorset. That Richard's excitement at Kennington's arrival was almost unbridled is therefore understandable.

Curious in both style and content, Kennington's letter raises more questions than it provides answers about Richard Stevens. Although it does make a number of otherwise fascinating observations. Chief among them, perhaps, is that "...he never once mentioned his wife or son". This is a statement made without context within the letter itself, but it may well be that it was in response to one from Mr Stevens, and in which he may have asked specific questions of Kennington. However, it certainly points up the estrangement which existed between Richard and his wife at this time. What cannot be ignored, either, are the expressions of an extreme closeness between Kennington and Richard and what was clearly an extraordinary bond. Of course, this could just have been born out of the pair being kindred spirits. That, and the T E Lawrence 'connection'. On the other hand, some might read into this letter that there could well have been something rather more than just friendship between the two. That said, there is nothing definitively to suggest anything of such a nature, and no evidence at all that either man was so inclined. However, it is easy to 'construct' such a scenario from this letter given references to 'John' (almost certainly John Simpson who was known to be gay), Epstein the artist (who wasn't apparently gay but had certain leanings) and, of course, his closeness to Lawrence of Arabia whose sexuality is now in little doubt. And then, of course, the frequent references to oddness, which Kennington sometimes placed in inverted commas. It would not be unreasonable to ask: was this a euphemism?

In his frequent references to Richard being 'odd' we could perhaps look at this as an expression of somebody who was special or different, and one who was apart from all the others; eccentricity might, perhaps, be what he was trying to convey. And eccentricity would almost certainly be a description which could be made of either man. In any event, it would seem most unlikely that Kennington would be writing to a bereaved father indicating something of his late son's predilections. Unless, of course, his father was also in on the 'secret'? After all, here was a bohemian, avant-garde and somewhat 'liberal' family who were not uncomfortable with matters sexual which, for other families of the time, would have been taboo to even discuss. At that time, of course, sexual orientations other than heterosexual ones were neither socially toler-ated nor legal, and so had to be kept very much under wraps and merely alluded to. Either way, and if this is what Kennington was trying to convey, it is something which is of little or no consequence in the twenty-first century – although it was, of course, of significant consequence then. In the story of Richard Stevens, then, it might otherwise be an irrelevance were it not for the curious references in Eric Kennington's letter.

Kennington's observations, for the large part, merely confirm all else we know about the man. That is, with one exception.

Along with the fable about Richard's wife and children being killed in the Blitz (or various permutations of the same tale), we are also told in Kennington's letter that: 'Of course, he was entirely without malice towards the enemy'. It is a statement which flies in the face of just about every single source of information about Richard and his psyche. And yet, in a letter from a man who knew him better than most, we have a de-finitive statement which simply turns that belief about him on its head. It is impossible to do anything other than accept at face value what Kennington says. How, though, do we then explain the picture which was painted of Richard – and never countered by Richard himself – that he held a deep-seated bitterness towards his enemy? It was also something commented on by his brother, James:

> "Hatred implies that if he met the pilot of a bomber he shot down, he would still want to kill him. I don't think he was ever like that, and as a family we never 'did' hatred. I think it was more that he saw the regime as something evil that must be destroyed. And their bomber aircraft flying over his coun-try, trying to destroy it and his people, that was just too much. So, anybody who came overhead had to be stopped and destroyed. It was as simple as that. I just feel that this: 'He blindly hated Jerries' line is a bit over-exagger-ated. After all, most people in Britain did to a greater or lesser extent. And in that regard, Dick was no different to anyone else."

Again, one can only conclude that this persona was all part of the public image which he wanted to put out in the public domain about his *raison d'être*, and that it suited him for others to believe his 'hatred' had come about from the death of his family at the hands of the Luftwaffe and drove him on. For the news media of the day, it was a dream of a story. And why let the facts get in the way of a good story?

Truly, then, Richard Playne Stevens was much like his hero T E Lawrence: an enigma. And it seems likely that he himself did much to encourage such an enigmatic status. Again, a trait very much in the mould of Lawrence himself.

When they packed up Richard Stevens' few private possessions at RAF Manston to send them home to his family, a well-thumbed copy of *Seven Pillars of Wisdom* was among his belongings. It was found open at a page with one sentence faintly under-lined in pencil: 'I wrote my will across the sky, in stars.'

Portrait of Richard Playne Stevens, DSO, DFC & Bar by Eric Kennington.

Chapter Ten

SOME DISCERN SPIRITS

There are a number of misconceptions relating to the life and RAF career of Richard Playne Stevens which have persisted across the years. Indeed, a good many of those myths and fables have become so well established that the folklore they actually represent has been repeated time and again by authors and researchers and ultimately presented as 'fact'. In part, this is probably due to the dearth of primary source material hitherto available on Richard and a consequent reliance on what are generally unreliable published sources. All of this started, of course, in the wartime works of H E Bates, although Sylvia Barbanell's book, *Some Discern Spirits* (London Psychic Press, 1944), somewhat bizarrely added to the mythology of 'Dick' Stevens. Not least of all, perhaps, because of the involvement of none other than Air Chief Marshal Sir Hugh Dowding in what was a slightly bizarre study of work by a renowned medium, Estelle Roberts.

The medium, Estelle Roberts, who claimed contact with Richard after his death and gave the family false 'information' as to the circumstances of his demise.

Dowding, for all his brilliance in leadership of RAF Fighter Command during the Battle of Britain, was an adherent to the notion of the spirit world and the ability to communicate with those of 'The Few' who had lost their lives. Bizarrely, he was also a believer in the existence of fairies. In the context of *Some Discern Spirits*, however, it was particularly the mention of Richard as a Battle of Britain pilot which has added fuel to the fire of suggestions that he had indeed flown in that battle. As we have already seen, that was not the case. However, and setting aside the more than highly questionable element of spiritualism, some credibility (if 'credibility' is the right word in this context) was attached to Dowding's apparent agreement in Barbanell's book that Richard was, indeed, one of his Battle of Britain 'Few'. Elements of Barbanell's account, however, do at least otherwise dispel the widely held belief that he was driven to bring down German raiders because his wife and children had all been killed during the Blitz.

In the book, we are told that Richard's widow attended a seance during 1942 along with Dowding. That much, at least, is factual. But the representation of all else that followed is at best fanciful and, at worst, the fabrication of a psychic crank. Nevertheless, and for all of that, the examination of what allegedly transpired at the seance in question is appropriate. It also allows us the opportunity to dispel any suggestion that Richard was a Battle of Britain pilot; that is, that he had served on an accredited RAF Fighter Command squadron between 10 July and 31 October 1940 and flown at least one operational sortie. He hadn't. However, comment apparently attributed to Dowding by Barbanell appears to suggest otherwise.

Setting the scene for the alleged manifestation of Richard's spirit at Estelle Roberts' gathering, Barbanell gives the following account:

> "Red Cloud [Roberts' spirit guide] stated that the next communicator would need the help of the sitters. This request from the guide usually means that a spirit has not spoken before in the direct voice. Through the trumpet we heard: 'Hullo. Am I down to earth yet? I want to talk to my wife...Dick Stevens...You are sitting next to my chief.'
>
> "The spirit speaker was 'Cat's Eyes' Stevens, the famous Battle of Britain fighter pilot, returning to his wife who sat beside Lord Dowding.
>
> "You remember me?" Stevens asked his old chief. "Of course I do," replied Lord Dowding."

In fact, and while Dowding may have *later* heard of Richard by reputation, Pilot Officer Stevens had joined 151 Squadron, Fighter Command, as a junior on 29 November 1940, five days after Dowding had been removed as C-in-C of RAF Fighter Command. It is wholly impossible that Richard Stevens, then an unknown junior officer who had yet to join an operational squadron, would have been known to Dowding at the time of the latter's command. Despite the dubious origin of the suggestion that he was a Battle of Britain pilot, it is a suggestion which appears to have been taken at face value by at least some researchers in post-war years, researchers who 'established' R P Stevens as a Battle of Britain pilot and might well have used Dowding's apparent confirmation of the fact as exactly that. But let us examine the real facts, far removed from the weird world of psychics and mediums which Dowding sometimes inhabited, and to look instead at how Richard Stevens' name was originally included on the Battle of Britain roll.

The initial work of compiling a list of all Battle of Britain participants was carried out by the late Flight Lieutenant John Holloway between 1955 and 1969. Surprisingly, up until that time, there was no publicly available nominal published roll of accredited participants and Holloway undertook to redress that omission and to present com-

Air Chief Marshal Sir Hugh Dowding.

memorative albums to Battle of Britain aircrew or their next of kin. It was a labour of love, but one which was conducted against a backdrop of often confusing or incomplete information. Surprisingly, no central 'official' roll was held by the Ministry of Defence or the RAF's Air Historical Branch, although it was obviously the case that individual airmen's records of service could be interrogated by the issuing authority to determine whether or not that man qualified under the relevant criteria as Battle of Britain aircrew, thus being entitled to the Battle of Britain clasp to his 1939-1945 Star. Upon such an award depended membership (for survivors) of the Battle of Britain Fighter Association and inclusion on any nominal roll.

Although it is difficult to determine exactly what happened when making the initial conclusion that R P Stevens served as a Battle of Britain pilot, it would appear to be the case that a certain Sergeant Stevens (with no recorded initials) was posted to 151 Squadron at RAF Digby on 4 September 1940. Then, just one week later, on 11 September, that same man is recorded in the squadron's operations record book as having been posted away. Coincidentally, of course, 151 Squadron was the squadron to which Richard Playne Stevens was ultimately assigned in November, and it seems likely that John Holloway noted the arrival of this Sergeant Stevens on the squadron, failed to note his subsequent posting out, and then simply assumed that this Stevens and R P Stevens must be one and the same man – especially in view of the common link with 151 Squadron. In fact, at this precise time, R P Stevens *was* a sergeant – not yet having been commissioned. So, initially but incorrectly, Richard Playne Stevens came to be listed as a Battle of Britain pilot.

In published sources, that error was compounded. First, in *Narrow Margin* (Wood and Dempster, Hutchinson & Company, 1961) and then in *Battle over Britain* (Mason, McWhirter Twins, 1969) followed by *Battle of Britain Then and Now* (Ramsey, After the Battle, 1980). All these books ran a Battle of Britain roll, with the published information based largely on Holloway's work.

In *Narrow Margin*, Richard is actually shown as Pilot Officer R P Stevens of 151 Squadron and that he was later killed. Mason, however, specifically lists Stevens as Sergeant R P Stevens who joined the squadron on 4 September 1940 (see above), was killed after the battle and was subsequently awarded the DSO, DFC and Bar. Clearly, this is intended to represent our Richard Playne Stevens. As for Winston Ramsey's superb work on the Battle of Britain, this again lists Pilot Officer R P Stevens, 151 Squadron. The same error was latter replicated by Kenneth G Wynn in the first editions of his seminal *Men of The Battle of Britain* (Gliddon Books, 1989), with all the varied and repeated errors picked up by other writers who were clearly using these different works as reference sources.

What we now know, of course, is that Richard Playne Stevens did not join 151 Squadron until 29 November 1940, too late to qualify as a Battle of Britain pilot. And this was certainly too late for Dowding to have even been aware of his existence, or to have thought that he was part of RAF Fighter Command's establishment at the material time of his command.

According to Barbanell, however, the seance was held before Richard's DSO was presented to his widow, Mabel. We know that that ceremony took place at Buckingham Palace on 23 June 1942, and so the event where Estelle Roberts supposedly invoked the spirit of 'Dick' Stevens must have been at some time prior to that, although Barbanell further states that Richard had told Mabel (through the medium) that: "You will be going to get a medal for me soon." Given that the *London Gazette* citation for the award of DSO was dated 12 December 1941 (three days before his death on 15 December), and the medal was presented just over six months later, it can hardly have been

Portrait of the airman—part of Eric Kennington's picture, "Night Flyer."

A number of period newspaper cuttings which, variously, gave misleading information about Richard's loss. It seems likely that Roberts had gleaned some detail from such reports, repeating the errors as she fed the misinformation into her seance.

necessary for a medium to 'reveal' to Mabel Stevens the rather less than surprising detail of the impending presentation ceremony.

It is, of course, hardly necessary to analyse or comment in any further detail on the additional revelations of 'Red Cloud', purportedly coming from Richard himself. Suffice to say, that additional snippets from this most peculiar of seances seem to have crept into the established narrative of Richard Playne Stevens' story, and it is as well to counter those once-and-for-all.

In her book, and allegedly avowed by Dowding himself, Barbanell tells us that Richard's demise had apparently taken place in daylight during operations off the Dutch coast. This, of course, is complete nonsense and it is something which was almost cer-

tainly drawn from the same version of events about his death which appeared in at
least one newspaper of the period, although it was also a 'revelation' made during the
seance. It must have simply been the case that the medium had read this piece of misleading information in the press and used it for her own purposes.

Barbanell further goes on to state that he radioed he had engine problems and, if
necessary, he would bale out over Holland. Then, nothing further was heard from him.
That version of events, however, is not borne out by Group Captain Tom Gleave's very
clear recall of events that night, nor by the recollections of 'Dickie' Bird who was also
at Manston the same night. Both would have surely known about any radioed message
about 'engine problems'. According to Estelle Roberts, however, Richard went on to
tell how that he had been shot down by a German aircraft (conflicting with the engine
failure version of events), that he had baled out but that his parachute got caught on
the wing. Again, none of those things are true. As we have seen, it is far more likely that
Richard simply flew into the ground, in darkness, whilst attacking unsuspecting German aircraft in the landing pattern at Gilze-Rijen airfield. And given we can now conclude that he most likely added to his 'kill' score just prior to crashing, it is somewhat
surprising that the 'spirit' which made itself known to the seance failed to mention this
more than significant fact!

According to the medium's further revelations, only pieces of his aircraft were found
beside an otherwise unidentified
body. Identification, it is claimed,
that was only possible when the aircraft itself could be identified. This
was allegedly achieved, or helped, by
the discovery of a piece of red tape on
what was left of the Hurricane. Richard, it was said by Barbanell, had a
pathological contempt of officialdom
(or 'red tape') and the red tape on his
aeroplane was to remind others of
this fact. Given that Barbanell's book
would have clearly been read, eventually, by Mabel Stevens it is certainly tempting to consider that the 'red
tape' marking may have a ring of truth
about it.

How such information might have
been 'known' to Roberts, however, is
unclear – although through a method
known as 'cold readings', psychics and

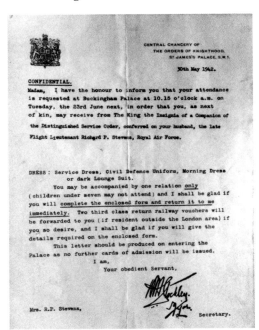

*Mabel Stevens' invitation to attend at Buckingham
Palace to receive her late husband's DSO.*

mediums commonly employ high-probability guesses, quickly picking up on signals or cues as to whether they are in the right direction or not. Then, through reinforcing chance connections, they quickly move deftly on from any missed guesses – the whole process often drawing in the person seeking contact with the spirit world through 'confirmation bias'. Such a condition will often exist in emotionally receptive individuals. And in the case of Richard Stevens, his frequent contempt of authority was not exactly unknown.

Given his predilection as something of a maverick, a rebel, and for sometimes having unusual markings on his aircraft, the red tape story might well be true. And we do know that a red question mark adorned the port engine cowling of his Hurricane – a marking which could easily have been fashioned from red adhesive tape, perhaps? What cannot be true, however, is that the Germans – in 1941 – would have used any such 'red tape' marking on his aircraft as an aid to his identification. In any event, they wouldn't have needed to. Richard would have had identity discs, named clothing and probably other means by which to identify his body formally.

Photographic evidence clearly shows his Hurricane relatively intact – and not comprising 'only pieces' as Estelle Roberts had mystically maintained. It is also known that his body was still in the cockpit and not 'nearby', his parachute still attached to him and in its pack rather than 'caught on the wing'.

Certainly, it must be somewhat unusual to even consider looking at what most would regard as lunatic ramblings emanating from a wartime seance. Yet the story of Richard Playne Stevens is anything but usual and the seance story undeniably forms part of the narrative. It is also a tale into which is woven the somewhat surreal participation of none other than Air Chief Marshal Sir Hugh Dowding. Moreover, the involvement of Estelle Roberts the spiritualist points up the raw grief and distress of families who had lost loved ones and who wanted to seek means – any means – by which they might derive some comfort and what we would now call closure. Reaching out to a medium for contact beyond the so-called 'gossamer veil' was a far from uncommon event at that time. In the case of Mabel Stevens' participation in the seance, however, it might also suggest a closeness to her late husband that was evidently not reciprocated by Richard Stevens during his lifetime.

Incidentally to illustrate the popularity of psychic events and seances during the Second World War, the notorious case of Helen Duncan and HMS *Barham* should be borne in mind. In that episode, which somewhat bizarrely resulted in one of the last trials in Britain under the Witchcraft Act of 1735, Duncan 'revealed' the loss of *Barham* and the deaths of 862 crew members after it had been sunk in the Mediterranean in November 1941. The seance was held in early 1942 (the same time frame as the Stevens seance) at which time the news of *Barham*'s sinking had been publicly withheld although next-of-kin had been notified. Given that the seance was held in Portsmouth, the *Barham*'s home port, it is not surprising that she had picked up gossip about the disaster. Nevertheless, Helen Duncan was jailed for nine months. Similarly, Jane Rebecca Yorke of Forest Gate, London, was also prosecuted under the act in 1944, for "...defrauding the public by exploiting wartime fears". During seances, undercover police were told to ask her about non-existent family members, and Yorke provided elaborate details which she claimed had been provided by her spirit guide. This included telling an officer that his non-existent brother had been burned alive on a bombing mission. Yorke was fined £5.00 and bound over on the condition of good behaviour.

Despite the case against both Duncan and Yorke, Estelle Roberts escaped prosecution or legal intervention although it is clear that both she, and Dowding, were probably sailing pretty close to the wind, legally speaking, in dabbling in the 'summoning' of Richard Stevens and others – albeit that Churchill, when hearing of the Helen Duncan case, complained to the Home Secretary, Herbert Morrison, about the waste of time and resources expended on "obsolete tomfoolery".

In his life and career, the 'Lone Wolf' was nothing if not an enigmatic character. In death – and figuratively speaking from 'beyond the grave' – he continued to carry with him a degree of mystery and intrigue. Feeding into this, of course, has hitherto been the lack of any reliable primary source reference material and a general acceptance that he had flown in the Battle of Britain, that his wife and children were killed during the Blitz[11] and the possibly flawed belief that he harboured a deep-seated hatred of Germans arising from that supposed tragedy.

The final word on Richard Playne Stevens, however, should not rest with the weirdness emanating from a medium, but from the author H E Bates:

"He went off to do it in the twilight of a winter evening. The time between departure and return, for a Hurricane, is not long. The time went by and the short margin of time behind it went by too until it became clear that the anger, the hatred and the desire for revenge had been dissipated at last.

"He is dead now – you are the living.

"His was the sky – yours is the earth because of him."

H E Bates.

---

11   In fact, Richard's widow, Olive Mabel Stevens, died in Hove, East Sussex, on 3 August 1987. His son, the surviving twin, John Lawrence Stevens died in Taranaki, New Zealand.

The war memorial at Hurspierpoint College where Richard Stevens is remembered. He went from being a singularly unremarkable student to one of the RAF's most notable 'aces' and the most famous war hero on the college's roll.

APPENDIX ONE
RECORD OF SERVICE

Flight Lieutenant Richard Playne Stevens DSO, DFC & Bar (87639)	
Date of Birth	11th September 1909
PREVIOUS SERVICE	
Enlisted as 740527 aircraftman class 2 / under training pilot	26 July 1937
Sergeant	27 July 1937
Remustered pilot	25 May 1938
Discharged on appointment to commission	3 November 1940
APPOINTMENTS AND PROMOTIONS	
Granted commission as pilot officer on probation in the General Duties	
Branch of the RAF Volunteer Reserve for duration of hostilities	4 November 1940
Confirmed in appointment and promoted flying officer (war substantive)	4 November 1941
Acting flight lieutenant	12 November 1941
Death presumed	15 December 1941
POSTINGS	
3 Personnel Transit Centre, West Drayton	10 April 1940
110 Anti-Aircraft Wing, Ringway	10 April 1940
6 Anti-Aircraft Co-Operation Unit	29 June 1940
56 Operational Training Unit	29 October 1940
151 Squadron	6 November 1940
253 Squadron[12]	12 November 1941
No 1 Depot RAF / missing / non-effective (flying battle)	15 December 1941
Further details recorded include:	
North East Airways 1938 – 39[13]	
Wrightways Ltd 1939 – 40	
Training Periods: (Redhill)	30 July to 18 August 1937
	1 October to 26 October 1937

Physical description:			
5ft 9ins	Hair: Mouse	Eyes: Blue	Complexion: Fresh

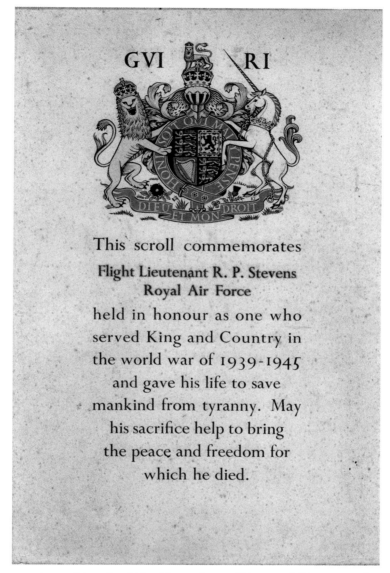

GVI RI

This scroll commemorates

Flight Lieutenant R. P. Stevens
Royal Air Force

held in honour as one who
served King and Country in
the world war of 1939-1945
and gave his life to save
mankind from tyranny. May
his sacrifice help to bring
the peace and freedom for
which he died.

The commemorative scroll issued to Richard Stevens' next-of-kin to mark his service and sacrifice to King and country.

12   Richard's posting to 253 Squadron on 12 November 1941 was at a time when the squadron were based at RAF Hibaldstow. However, he was immediately sent on detachment to RAF Manston to develop night-intruding methods.

13   Employment with 'North East Airways' is not corroborated by available evidence. Further, his employment with Air Couriers Ltd. is not mentioned on his RAF Record of Service sheets.

APPENDIX TWO
AWARDS AND DECORATIONS

The following gallantry awards and service decorations were granted to Flight Lieutenant R P Stevens in recognition of his service:

Distinguished Flying Cross

The *London Gazette* citation, published on 4 February 1941, for the award of DFC read as follows:

> "This officer has performed outstanding work on nightfighting operations during recent weeks. One night in January, 1941, he shot down two hostile aircraft in the London area. In both these engagements he chased the enemy over 100 miles before destroying each at extremely short range. In one instance he followed the enemy aircraft almost to ground level from 30,000 feet. He has shown the utmost keenness and determination for operations in all conditions of weather."

Bar to Distinguished Flying Cross

The *London Gazette* citation, published on 29 April 1941, for a Bar to the DFC read as follows:

> "This officer has done particularly outstanding work with his squadron on night operations and has on three occasions shot down two enemy aircraft in one night. Pilot Officer Stevens shows a great determination to attack the enemy and is prepared to fly under the most difficult weather conditions. His courage, determination, thoroughness and skill have set an excellent example to his unit."

Both the DFC and the Bar to the DFC were awarded to Richard Playne Stevens by His Majesty King George VI in an investiture at Buckingham Palace on 20 May 1941.

Distinguished Service Order

The *London Gazette* citation, published on 12 December 1941, for the award of DSO read as follows:

> "This officer has shown himself to be a fearless and outstanding nightfighter

pilot. One night in October 1941, flying at sea level, he intercepted a Junkers 88 off the East Anglian coast. The raider immediately turned and flew towards the continent at maximum speed, but Flight Lieutenant Stevens gave chase and slowly overhauled it. The raider then opened fire with his guns and began to drop his bombs singly. Columns of water were shot up as a result of the explosions, but Flight Lieutenant Stevens swerved round them and, closing in to short range, shot down the enemy aircraft at almost sea level. He has destroyed at least 14 hostile aircraft at night."

Flight Lieutenant Richard Playne Stevens did not live to receive this award in person. Instead, it was handed to his widow, Olive Mabel Stevens, by His Majesty King George VI at a Buckingham Palace investiture on Tuesday, 23 June 1942

Flight Lieutenant R P Stevens, DSO, DFC & Bar was also entitled to the following service medals:

1939 – 1945 Star
Air Crew Europe Star
War Medal
Defence Medal

APPENDIX THREE
LIST OF VICTORY CLAIMS

For simplicity, the official victory claims for Flight Lieutenant R P Stevens DSO DFC & Bar are shown below in a format which gives the victories expressed as taking place on the night between the two dates shown:

	1941	
15/16 January	Dornier 17	Brentwood, Essex
15/16 January	Heinkel 111	Off Canvey Island
12/13 March	Junkers 88 (Probable)	East of Aldeburgh
8/9 April	Heinkel 111	Wellesbourne
8/9 April	Heinkel 111	Peckleton
10/11 April	Junkers 88	Murcott
10/11 April	Heinkel 111	Kettering
19/20 April	Heinkel 111	Stockbury
8/9 May	Heinkel 111	East of Hull
8/9 May	Heinkel 111	East of Hull
10/11 May	Heinkel 111	Withyham
10/11 May	Heinkel 111 (Probable)	London area
13/14 June	Heinkel 111	Halstow
20/21 June	Heinkel 111 (Damaged)	East of Winterton
29/30 June	Junkers 88	ENE of Happisburgh
5/6 July	Junkers 88	Off Sheringham
16/17 October	Junkers 88	Off Winterton
22/23 October	Junkers 88 (Half share)	Market Drayton
15/16 December[14]	Junkers 88	Gilze-Rijen

14   The victory that we now know was secured over Gilze-Rijen on the night that Flight Lieutenant R P Stevens was killed was not on his list of official victories, although post-war research has clearly identified this as a 'kill' which can certainly be attributed to him.

This unofficially increases his score, therefore, to 15 ½ aircraft destroyed, two aircraft probably destroyed and one damaged.

APPENDIX FOUR
HURRICANE IIc Z3465

The following detail is recorded on the Air Ministry From 78, or Aircraft Record Card, for Hurricane IIc in which Flight Lieutenant Stevens was lost:

Built by Hawkers under contract 62305/39.
Rolls-Royce Merlin XX engine
Delivered to 27 MU on 11 May 1941
To 151 Squadron on 1 June 1941
To 253 Squadron on 20 November 1941
Missing on 15 December 1941
Struck off Charge on 15 December 1941

NB: Some sources suggest this aircraft carried the fuselage codes TL – A, although witnesses who served at Manston stated that the aircraft carried no fuselage code letters at the time of its loss.

An Accident Record Card (RAF Form 1180) was also raised for Z3465, presumably on the basis that at the time of its disappearance the circumstances of the aircraft's loss remained unknown.

APPENDIX FIVE
TRIBUTES

Secretary of State for Air, Sir Archibald Sinclair:

"One of the greatest nightfighter pilots who ever fought in Fighter Command."

Air Vice-Marshal 'Johnnie'Johnson DSO & two bars, DFC & bar:

"He was quite fearless and attacked his opponents at such close range that on some occasions his Hurricane was badly damaged by the force of the explosion. His end was inevitable, and after destroying at least fourteen enemy aircraft at night he failed to return from a patrol over enemy territory and was never seen again. We have the fondest memories of him."

Air Vice-Marshal B E Embry DSO, AFC, ADC:

"Flight Lieutenant R P Stevens served under my direct command from December 1940 until November 1941. During that time, he showed outstanding gallantry in night operations against the enemy in the defence of this country. It was during this period that he received his three decorations which is a clear indication of the high value placed on his work by His Majesty the King and the Commander-in-Chief, Fighter Command.

"It was during 1941 that the great night battle of this country took place and I do not hesitate to say that the example set by the late Flight Lieutenant Stevens and his high standard of courage and skill as a nightfighter pilot contributed to the final defeat of the enemy at night."

Air Vice-Marshal W B Callaway CBE, AFC (HQ Fighter Command):

"This officer was employed intensively on nightfighting operations when night-flying technique was in its infancy and risks were far greater than they are today. He was quite without fear and operated against the enemy under weather conditions which would have been quite impossible for the average pilot."

Air Vice-Marshal Sir Douglas Evill GBE, KCB, DSC, AFC (Vice-Chief of the Air Staff, 1943):

"His great gallantry and remarkable successes achieved largely at a period when our methods of night defence were in an early stage of development were of the highest possible value to the Command and to the country. Not only did he destroy many enemy aircraft at night under conditions and often in weather which seemed prohibitive, but in so doing he set up a standard of flying and leadership which inspired other pilots to higher standards of efficiency and success."

Group Captain Desmond Scott DSO, OBE, DFC & bar:

"Brave as a lion, and indefatigable. A tremendous example to all who knew him. He was my idol and his loss was a severe blow."

Daily Herald:

"The RAF's greatest nightfighter pilot has been killed."

Unattributed fellow pilot:

"He looked on the whole country as his operational parish. He was also the greatest nightfighter pilot of all time."

BIBLIOGRAPHY

Chisholm, Roderick, *Cover of Darkness*, Chatto & Windus, 1953
Goss, Chris, *The Luftwaffe's Blitz*, Crecy, 2000
Halley, James J., *The Squadrons of the Royal Air Force & Commonwealth 1918–1988*, Air Britain, 1988
Helmore, Group Captain W., *Air Commentary*, George Allen & Unwin, 1942
Kennington, Eric, *Drawing the RAF*, Oxford University Press, 1942
Lake, Alan, *Flying Units of the RAF*, Airlife, 1999
Mason, Francis K., *Battle over Britain*, McWhirter Twins, 1969
Mason, Francis K., *The Hawker Hurricane*, Crecy, 2001
Masters, David, *So Few – The Immortal Record of the RAF*, Eyre & Spottiswoode, 1941
Parker, Nigel, *Luftwaffe Crash Archive (Vols 7,8 & 9)*, Red Kite, 2013/2017
Ramsey, Winston G., *The Blitz Then And Now – Volume 2*, After The Battle, 1990
Rawnsley, C. F. and Wright, Robert, *Night Fighter*, Collins, 1957
Shores, Christopher and Williams, Clive, *Aces High*, Grub Street, 1994
Wood, Derek with Dempster, Derek, *The Narrow Margin*, Hutchinson & Co, 1961

INDEX